Local Approaches to Environmental Compliance

*Japanese Case Studies and
Lessons for Developing Countries*

Edited by

Adriana Bianchi
Wilfrido Cruz
Masahisa Nakamura

The World Bank
Washington, D.C.

Contents

Foreword

By any standard, Japan has made remarkable progress in urban and industrial environmental management. It has successfully handled the massive pollution caused by its rapid industrial expansion after World War II and now effectively integrates environmental protection and clean technologies into industrial processes and urban transportation. Although technological improvements clearly play an important role in Japan's response to environmental problems, they comprise only a portion of the process that has led to significant reductions in environmental pollution and land degradation. Institutional coordination, economic incentives, and local involvement also play important roles in determining environmental protection measures and in ensuring environmental compliance and enforcement.

As developing countries struggle to forge effective partnerships between national government agencies on the one hand and industry and local communities on the other, Japan's history of urban and industrial management can provide useful examples of government-industry-community cooperation. Although many problems remain, the lessons from Japan's experience in developing and implementing strict but practical environmental standards appear to be highly relevant to developing countries. Indeed, an exchange of environmental management experiences with Japan could be very productive for these countries. There is increasing recognition among policymakers that industrial and urban expansion will lead to costly environmental problems in the near future unless management interventions are initiated soon.

This book has two specific objectives: (1) to highlight key features of Japan's approach to the development and enforcement of environmental standards (namely, local government involvement, community participation, and private industry initiatives) and (2) to identify aspects of this experience that are relevant to developing countries. Case studies from Japan and reviews from developing countries were commissioned to address these goals. Their findings were also discussed in workshops involving developing country participants and resource persons from Japan.

The World Bank Institute was fortunate to have the cooperation and assistance of numerous environmental organizations and agencies, including the Ministry of the Environment and the International Lake Environment Committee (based in the Shiga Prefecture). Financial assistance to the various activities mentioned above was provided by the government of Japan. This helped WBI to assemble an excellent group of resource persons from Japan to prepare the case studies. In addition, environmental officials and specialists from developing countries in East Asia reviewed the case studies, focusing on the aspects that would be most relevant to their own countries.

Frannie A. Léautier
Vice President
World Bank Institute

Preface

Japan has been a leader in the use of technological improvements to help control problems of urban and industrial pollution. However, Japan's progress in improving air and water quality and in managing solid and hazardous wastes occurred within a certain policy, institutional, and local context that made possible these technological improvements. Thus, the focus of this book, and of the World Bank Institute (WBI) workshops in Manila and in Kusatsu in 2002, is on local participation, economic policy, and institutional issues, rather than on technological improvements per se. The case studies and reviews emphasized the following factors that contribute to effective environmental regulation and compliance mechanisms at the local level:

- the involvement of local authorities;
- the influence of community-based constituencies and private industry;
- the availability of technology and management capacity; and
- the role of favorable economic conditions and financial support to industry.

In addition, a number of characteristics of Japanese society help explain Japan's success in urban environmental management. (Some of these underlying characteristics are highly relevant for developing countries. Indeed, the development community widely encourages them, apart from their beneficial impact on environmental considerations.) Such factors include decentralization of decisionmaking; an efficient and democratic local government; a competent labor force; a well-educated and articulate population; and an active press. Although they are necessary conditions for sustainable environmental management, these factors are not directly in the scope of environmental agencies. Thus, the reviews by developing-country resource persons focused on how Japanese approaches accommodated these other factors and how the environmental strategies in their own countries could benefit from the experience of Japan.

Chapter 1 of this book synthesizes the key elements of the Japanese experience that are relevant for developing countries. In particular, the political, economic, and institutional constraints to environmental compliance and enforcement are discussed. Differences and similarities between Japan's past experience and current conditions in developing countries are explored. Chapters 2 through 6 present case studies that detail how Japan has managed air, water, and solid waste problems. Conclusions regarding the relevance of the Japanese experience to East Asian developing countries and "emerging lessons" are presented in the final chapter.

Acknowledgments

The editors and contributors are grateful to everyone who helped in the preparation of this book. The publication effort was part of a broader World Bank Institute capacity-building program entitled "Practical Approaches to Environmental Regulation, Compliance, and Enforcement," which received financial support from the Japanese government.

We acknowledge the important contributions of developing-country resource persons who served as reviewers for the Japanese case studies: Ruben D. Almendras, Nam Thang Do, Rosa Vivien Ratnawati, Indra Mufardi Roesli, Supat Wangwongwatana, Budi Widianarko, and Jianyu Zhang. Summaries of their reviews are presented in Appendix A. We also thank the numerous individuals, both from the World Bank and other development and environmental agencies, who assisted in the preparation of these program activities, especially the following: Pamela Gallares-Opus, regional director for Southeast Asia of the International Council for Local Environmental Initiatives (ICLEI), and Akiko Murano of the secretariat of the International Lake Environment Committee (ILEC).

We are grateful to Laura Tlaiye, Michele de Nevers, John Didier, and Chiharu Ima of the World Bank Institute for their support during the various phases of preparation and completion of WBI's program on "Practical Approaches to Environmental Regulation, Compliance, and Enforcement." With regard to our cooperation with the Japan Ministry of the Environment, we are especially grateful to Kazuhiko Takemoto, deputy director-general of the Global Environment Bureau of the Ministry, for his help as an external adviser on this project. We also thank Michio Hashimoto, who is widely regarded as the father of environmentalism in Japan, for his helpful and insightful comments about the case studies. He was the first head of the Environment Agency in Japan and is now the president of the Overseas Environmental Cooperation Center in Tokyo.

During the publication phase, constructive suggestions were received from Hisakazu Kato and Colin Rees, the external reviewers for this book. We acknowledge the help of Adelaida Schwab for her technical reviews of the papers, Barbara de Boinville for her editing of the manuscript, and WBI staff (Nelvia Diaz, Teresa Argueta, and Maria Rosa Schwartz) for providing excellent administrative support during the various phases of the program.

Any remaining omissions or errors in the book are the sole responsibilities of the editors.

About the Editors and Contributors

THOMAS J. BALLATORE
Researcher
Research Division
International Lake Environment Committee
Kusatsu, Japan

ADRIANA BIANCHI
Senior Institutional Development Specialist
World Bank Institute
Washington, D.C.

WILFRIDO CRUZ
Consultant
World Bank Institute
Washington, D.C.

RYO FUJIKURA
Professor
Faculty of Humanity and Environment
Hosei University
Tokyo, Japan

SOO CHEOL LEE
Assistant Professor
Faculty of Economics
Nagoya Gakuin University
Nagoya, Japan

AKIHISA MORI
Professor
Graduate School of Global Environmental
    Studies
Kyoto University
Kyoto, Japan

VICTOR S. MUHANDIKI
Researcher
Research Division
International Lake Environment Committee
Kusatsu, Japan

MASAHISA NAKAMURA
Director
Lake Biwa Research Institute
Kusatsu, Japan

KAZUHIRO UETA
Professor
Graduate School of Economics and Global
    Environmental Studies
Kyoto University
Kyoto, Japan

1

Environmental Compliance:
Case Studies from Japan and Their Relevance
to East Asian Developing Countries

Adriana Bianchi, Wilfrido Cruz, and Masahisa Nakamura

Why have environmental regulations been so difficult to enforce in developing countries? The conventional answer, often repeated since the Rio de Janeiro summit on environmental management more than a decade ago, is that the necessary regulations exist for environmental protection; what is absent is implementation.

Constraints to Environmental Compliance and Enforcement

The principal obstacles to environmental compliance and enforcement in developing countries revolve around constraints that are political, economic, and institutional. As demonstrated in the Japanese case studies, effective responses have often required consensus and commitment at the local government and community levels. Although there are many instances when implementation is hindered by lack of technical skills or lack of the needed technology, the underlying constraints are rarely technological.

In fact, the technological facet of environmental compliance and enforcement in Japan is merely the ìtip of the iceberg.î As the case studies demonstrate, underlying this ìtipî are political, economic, and institutional factors. In Japan local government resources and community and private industry resources have been mobilized in the search for agreement on ways to implement remedial action.

The constraints to environmental compliance and enforcement, and the local initiatives to implement pollution management, constitute the framework for analyzing the relevance of Japanís experience to developing countries in this book. As noted earlier, the first type of constraint is political. Strong vested interests compete with each other and often resist environmental protection measures. Almost by definition, environmental problems are externalities; benefits from emissions (or overexploitation) accrue to an individual or to a small group, but the damages are borne by society at large. With regard to economic constraints and competing priorities, environmental management historically has played a minor role compared to promotion of industrial development in many countries. Thus, regulations in Japan were late, and even when they were enacted, implementation was limited.

In most developing countries, environmental agencies are relatively weak compared to trade and industry agencies and agricultural agencies. Because of these institutional constraints, environmental agencies in most developing countries are unable to build consensus to implement standards. Government agencies disagree on what should be done, and many are hostile to environmental regulation. Japanís experience speaks to these challenges, as the next section, a summary of the main findings of the case studies, makes clear.

Japan's Experience in Addressing Environmental Constraints

In Japan communities and private sector initiatives have played a significant role in promoting environmental enforcement and compliance. The Japanese experience underscores the importance of fostering community and private sector involvement and a clearer understanding of the role of government at the local and national levels. At the national level, an appropriate legal and regulatory framework is required. It is also important for the policy and economic incentives to be conducive to environmental management. At the local level, there is a need to improve the capacity of local government units and their pollution management agencies. Lastly, at the community or site level, private industry and community groups need to be better informed and organized to promote proactive implementation of environmental management programs. The experience of Japan is especially relevant in demonstrating the power of local communities to effect change.

This section presents the main findings of the five case studies presented in Chapters 2 through 6. The first case study describes the evolution of air pollution control in Japan. It focuses on local management efforts in selected cities. The second case study is on water pollution management at the national and local (or prefectural) levels. It highlights the development of water quality management at Lake Biwa, Japan's most important lake, located in the Shiga Prefecture. This discussion of water pollution programs at a broad level is complemented in the next chapter by the specific example of water pollution control by an individual factory. The intent of this third case study is to highlight the extent of remediation at the private industry level. The last two case studies—one on the implementation of the "soft loan" program to finance industrial investment in pollution control and the other on the contribution of a city's solid waste program to global environment goals—discuss economic incentives that can support environmental protection measures under changing environmental concerns for industry and local governments.

Successful Air Pollution Control in Japan: History and Implications

The case study by Ryo Fujikura (see Chapter 2) discusses Japan's legislative policies to address air pollution caused initially by the use of coal in factories in the 1960s and subsequently by the fuel switch to heavy oil, which led to sulfur oxide pollutants. Japan's rapid economic growth in the 1960s was achieved by the country's promotion of heavy industries. This economic expansion was attained, however, with limited consideration for the environment. Industrial activities caused serious air pollution in the country's major urban areas. Then, in the late 1960s and early 1970s, protests by citizens forced government officials to shift their focus from mere "economic development" to "pollution control." National policy was adjusted to emphasize antipollution measures, and this marked the beginning of the period known as "Japan's Pollution Miracle."

LEGISLATION FOR POLLUTION CONTROL. During the 1930s, Osaka was known as the "City of Smoke." Its very high levels of coal dust falls originated from factories in and around the city. Although two important regulations were passed at that time in response to citizens' protests, the weak regulatory enforcement, because of strong opposition from local businesses, and a lack of antipollution technology resulted in persistent pollution problems in Osaka. In Tokyo and Kitakyushu, dust falls and soot pollution from coal use in factories and homes were also creating environmental problems. Unlike in Tokyo, where residents strongly petitioned the local government to take appropriate measures to address the air pollution problem, in Kitakyushu residents regarded the black smoke as a "symbol of economic prosperity."

During the reconstruction era after World War II, major cities (such as Tokyo, Fukuoka, and Ube) passed ordinances for controlling coal dust and soot emissions from factories. These ordinances, like the regulations passed in Osaka, were largely ineffective for the same reasons. At the national level, the Ministry of Health and the Ministry of International Trade and Industry

(MITI) collaborated to draft a pollution control bill that took into account the health implications of poor air quality for local residents. However, local businesses blocked the introduction of the bill to the Diet.

During the 1960s, industries throughout Japan changed their energy source from domestic coal to heavy oil imported from the Middle East. Two main economic events influenced this change: strikes by coal mine workers (which resulted in higher coal prices and unstable supply) and the development of oil fields in the Middle East. The shift to heavy oil from coal shifted pollution concerns from particulates to sulfur oxides.

In 1967 the National Government passed the Basic Law of Pollution Control. Like the previous legislation for soot and smoke control passed at the national level, this bill accommodated the interests of the business sector. Environmental management was to be undertaken "in harmony with sound industrial development"—reflecting the strong influence of the business community on government decisions to implement less stringent pollution control measures. Nevertheless, the 1967 law established ambient environmental quality standards (EQSs) for sulfur oxides, which became critical in enforcing pollution control in Japan in succeeding years.

During the 1970s, the Pollution Control Diet Session was convened by Prime Minister E. Sato, and fourteen environmental conservation bills were passed. One of them established the Environment Agency of Japan, and the controversial provision harmonizing environmental management with sound industrial development was deleted from the 1967 law. These legislative developments occurred in response to citizens' growing environmental awareness and diminishing support for the Liberal Democratic Party (LDP). In some of Japan's major cities (for example, Yokohama, Tokyo, and Kawasaki), citizens elected Socialist Party members to replace LDP incumbents, believing that leftist politicians would do a better job in protecting the environment.

LOCAL APPROACHES TO COMPLIANCE AND ENFORCEMENT. Yokohama, Kitakyushu, Osaka, and Yokkaichi, four major industrial cities in Japan, used different approaches to control pollution from sulfur oxides. Yokohama City adopted an innovative approach based on pollution control agreements. Kitakyushu City achieved air pollution reduction through a combination of citizens' protests and pollution control agreements. In Osaka City success in pollution control was based on (a) traditional cooperation involving the municipal government, local residents, and the local business community and (b) the administrative guidance given to individual factories by the municipal government. In Yokkaichi City the local government resorted to direct pollution regulation after other efforts failed to reduce emissions significantly. The actions taken by four cities described below illustrate both the limits and the value of using local partnerships and common interests to manage pollution.

Yokohama City. In 1964 Ichio Asakata of the Socialist Party defeated the incumbent mayor, a member of the conservative Liberal Democratic Party (LDP). At the time local residents were convinced that the pro-business policies of LDP, both at the national and local government levels, were responsible for polluting the environment. Before the election there was a plan to establish a new coal-fired power plant at Isogo by the Electric Power Development Company (EPDC). The national government required that EPDC should purchase land from Tokyo Electric Company Ltd. as the site of the proposed power plant. For the land sale to take effect, the approval of the mayor was needed. Since the building of the coal power plant was a national policy, Mr. Asakata could not oppose the plan. The power plant would constitute a new tax base for the local government. Its construction also would be in the interest of local coal miners, supporters of the Socialist Party. Complicating the mayor's dilemma were protests by local residents who had become more vocal about their environmental concerns.

The conflict was resolved when the mayor granted EPDC the legal right to purchase land from Tokyo Electric, and EPDC, in exchange, accepted pollution control agreements (PCAs). Under these agreements, the municipal government required EPDC to (a) use low-sulfur coals from the Hokkaido mine in new power plants; (b) adopt the best available technologies to reduce sulfur oxides emissions; and (c) permit inspections by municipal government officials. In 1970 actual sulfur oxides emissions in Yokohama City were estimated at 60 tons per day, down from an estimated 300 tons per day in 1966.

Kitakyushu City. For years Kitakyushu residents had regarded the black smoke coming from the city's factories as a symbol of economic prosperity. The majority of local residents were factory workers or relatives of factory workers; many residents were employed by Yahata Works, Japan's largest iron mill. (Yahata Works later became part of the Nippon Steel Corporation.)

Local residents had kept quiet over a long period of time about the growing deterioration of air quality in Kitakyushu City. However, in the mid-1960s, local women organized groups to study pollution problems in their area. They did not directly challenge the factory owners, since these factories were their families' means of livelihood, but they petitioned the municipal government to enforce antipollution measures. These women backed their petitions with the results from their study, and they reported their study findings to the mass media. These actions helped inform the general public about the health hazards of air pollution, and they were essential in winning support from the municipal government.

Pollution became the most important issue in the 1971 mayoralty election. Fearful of losing popular support, the incumbent mayor of Kitakyushu City, G. Tani, undertook drastic pollution control measures: in 1970 he upgraded the eight-member Pollution Control Division to a twenty-two-member Pollution Control Department, and in 1971 he upgraded the department to a forty-seven-member Pollution Control Bureau. Local industries supported the mayor because they were convinced that, if he was defeated in the election, his leftist replacement would institute more stringent measures.

In 1970 the Fukuoka Prefectural Government, the Kitakyushu City Government, and major industries (thirty factories emitting 97 percent of the city's sulfur oxides) established the Joint Committee on Air Pollution Prevention in Kitakyushu. To meet national environmental standards by fiscal 1973, the municipal government concluded pollution control agreements with fifty-four factories based on agreements reached at the Joint Committee meeting.

There were other events that led to considerable reductions in sulfur oxides emissions both at the national and local levels. The oil shocks of the 1970s had forced Japanese industries to consider energy conservation measures, and by 1974 flue gas desulfurization technology was practicable. In Kitakyushu City about 42 percent of reductions in sulfur dioxide emissions in 1990 were due to switching to low-sulfur fuels in industries, 33 percent to energy savings and recycling, and 25 percent to flue gas desulfurization.

Osaka City. Through the traditional cooperation between the municipal government and local communities, the residents of Osaka had a "sense of ownership" of the city. Local residents and businesses looked upon the municipal government as their own organization for managing their communities. Consequently, they provided continuous financial donations to the city. The municipal government, in turn, provided support to local industries (for example, soft loans, especially to small-scale and medium-scale industries). This traditional cooperation between local government and local communities made the enforcement of industrial pollution control measures in Osaka City effective.

Through support from the municipal government, local businesses established the Soot and Smoke Prevention Cooperation Association at the ward level in 1958, and two years later they established the *Osaka Alliance* of the ward-level associations. Both organizations conducted an investigation into pollution control technologies and raised environmental awareness within the business community. Based on these efforts, the municipal government was able to provide administrative guidance to local factories without having to resort to legal requirements.

In turn, the municipal government prepared for public review an Administrative Guidance Plan based on scientific data. Local industries understood the importance of controlling air pollution, and they prepared their own antipollution plan. After consolidating information from government and industry sources, the municipal government issued emission reduction targets for individual factories and facilities. It was through this process that the municipal government succeeded in reducing air pollution in Osaka City.

Yokkaichi City. In the mid-1950s, Yokkaichi City was the site of the largest petrochemical complex in Asia. Pollution in residential areas in the vicinity of the complex was extremely serious, and in the early 1960s, numerous cases of asthma were reported there. The municipal government's initial response was to allocate a special budget of ten million yen to provide medical assistance to asthma patients. In 1963 MITI and the health ministry organized the Kurokawa Committee to identify pollution control measures for adoption by petrochemical factories. Since these factories strongly opposed any measures that would entail a switch to low-sulfur fuel, the committee recommended the installation of higher smoke stacks to disperse emissions. The Air Pollution Control Law of 1967 implemented this recommendation. By 1967 almost all of the factories in the petrochemical complex had installed stacks as high as 100 to 200 meters; the number of asthma patients, however, continued to increase. Some of them sued the factories for compensation for health damages and won. The court ordered the factories to pay the victims over 88 million yen.

Because of the limited impact of the preceding pollution control measures and because of the court decision, the prefectural government required petrochemical factories in the early 1970s to cut their sulfur oxides emissions. Total emissions control was introduced based on the Mie Prefecture Ordinance for Pollution Control. This measure included an interim target concentration—annual average of 0.025 parts per million (ppm) of SO_2—to be reached by 1974; a final target concentration (0.017 ppm) to be reached thereafter; fuel consumption at each factory not to exceed the 1973 consumption level; control of the sulfur content of fuel; and expansion of existing facilities and/or establishment of new ones to be subject to approval by the prefectural government. As a result of the total emissions control measure, annual sulfur oxide emissions in Yokkaichi City declined from over 100,000 tons in 1971 to 17,000 tons in 1975.

Water Management Standards and Environmental Compliance in Japan at the National and Prefectural Levels

The case study by Thomas J. Ballatore, Victor S. Muhandiki, and Masahisa Nakamura (see Chapter 3) focuses on the evolution of water quality standards in Japan at the national and local (prefectural) levels. It also reviews the major causes of water pollution in postwar Japan and legislation to resolve the water pollution problems in the country. Phosphorous discharged from industrial sources, causing eutrophication of the Lake Biwa watershed in the Shiga Prefecture, has been controlled successfully by efforts at the prefectural level. Using effluent data from 388 industrial dischargers, the authors analyze why firms have reduced their phosphorous effluents well below required standards.

CAUSES OF WATER POLLUTION. The three main causes of water pollution in postwar Japan are high population growth, rapid industrialization, and changes in land and resource use. From 1945 to 1975, Japan's population increased from 70 million people to 110 million. Japan became the fourth most densely populated country in the world, with 340 persons per square kilometer. In the years 1955 to 1973, Japan experienced some of the highest rates of economic growth in its history. Massive increases in labor productivity, a high domestic savings rate, and favorable international economic conditions contributed to annual GDP growth of over 10 percent. Rapid industrialization in the early postwar period, however, had led to a dramatic increase in environmental pollution.

Industrialization and population growth resulted in a shift from traditional lifestyles to more consumption-oriented lifestyles. Increases in per capita consumption and waste output, and drastic changes in resource use, had major adverse impacts on the environment. For example, in agricultural production the replacement of "night soil" by increased application of synthetic fertilizers—and the consequent discharge of night soil into waterways and of fertilizer runoff into rivers—seriously degraded Japan's water quality.

POLLUTION CONTROL AGREEMENTS (PCAs). Public discontent with the adverse effects of pollution markedly increased as the population's income and living standards rose sharply. Indeed, public discontent was the most important factor to influence Japan's legislative regulations and judicial measures for addressing environmental pollution. Pollution at the local level was dealt with successfully through pollution control agreements that involved participation by local residents, the business community, and local government officials. PCAs are the direct result of increased public awareness of the negative health effects of environmental pollution. As noted in the previous case study, the first PCA was between the city of Yokohama and an electric company; it was signed in 1964. Adoption of PCAs became widespread in the other major cities of Japan. There are several reasons, among them cultural mores, limited space to relocate businesses, as well as public shame and community pressure on polluters. Together these influences contributed to the success of PCAs in abating pollution at the local level. The total number of PCAs reached about 30,000 by the late 1990s.

Japan's water quality for the period 1971 through 2000 was analyzed separately for toxic pollutants—for example, lead, arsenic, cadmium, mercury, and cyanide—and for nontoxic pollutants—for example, biological oxygen demand (BOD) and chemical oxygen demand (COD). Nonconformity with ambient standards for discharges of regulated toxic substances from industries decreased significantly from 1971 to 1992. By 1992 the rate of nonconformity had fallen below 0.1 percent for most toxic substances. However, there was a sudden increase in nonconformity in 1993 due to (a) the addition of new substances to the regulated list and (b) the general tightening of standards. Japan has been less successful controlling nontoxic pollutants than in controlling toxic pollutants. Conformity with ambient standards for BOD and COD has not improved significantly since the 1970s, especially regarding the water quality of Japan's lakes and reservoirs. The Shiga Prefecture, located in central Japan and surrounding Lake Biwa, is an exception.

SHIGA PREFECTURE. By law, the ambient concentration of phosphorous (P) is required to be below 0.01 milligrams per liter (mg/l), and effluent standards have been developed (both at the national and prefectural levels) to control industrial and municipal point sources. The Shiga Prefecture imposed strict measures to improve water quality in Lake Biwa. For example, it banned P-containing detergents, it extended the collection area of the sewerage system, and it re-introduced natural reed beds around the lake.

The Water Pollution Control Law of 1970 is the statutory basis for national effluent standards. This law sets a minimum standard of environmental protection, but it contains provisions that allow prefectural governments to set stricter standards as needed. In the case of Shiga Prefecture, the national effluent standards were inadequate. In 1972 the Prefecture implemented an ordinance imposing stricter levels on COD, BOD, and suspended solid (SS) discharges from industrial facilities. In 1979 the Shiga Prefecture also passed the Eutrophication Prevention Ordinance (EPO) to regulate discharges of nitrogen and phosphorous.

The Water Pollution Control Law sets *concentration-based* standards for pollutants like phosphorous; however, eutrophication of water bodies depends on nutrient load. Consequently, the Lake

Law of 1984, which was modeled after Shiga's EPO of 1979, codifies the statutory basis for *load-based* standards to control eutrophication.

Spot inspections and self-monitoring are the main ways to monitor effluent quality throughout Japan. Water samples are taken during spot inspections conducted by the governor's office and sent to a laboratory for nutrient analysis. If the results of the spot inspection reveal a violation of the standards, the discharger is given the opportunity to explain its noncompliance. Self-monitoring data may be used in the process. If the violation is small, a "light warning" is issued. Otherwise, improvements in production technology may be required, or more stringent "administrative measures" may be imposed.

An analysis of spot inspections and monitoring data of 388 dischargers (food, textile, chemical, and other industries) in Shiga Prefecture showed that most dischargers had phosphorous effluents well below allowed levels. There are several possible reasons for this interesting finding. One is that variability in process efficiency has encouraged dischargers to factor into their effluent abatement decisions a margin of safety. Another is that some dischargers may have made investments in abatement equipment that is larger than needed. Others may have bought equipment in discrete sizes for more flexible control of effluent discharge. Finally, companies' sense of good will may have induced voluntary reduction of effluent levels.

Local Efforts to Control Water Pollution: A Case Study of a Metal-Plating Industry in the Shiga Prefecture

The case study by Victor S. Muhandiki, Thomas J. Ballatore, and Masahisa Nakamura (see Chapter 4) explores in detail pollution control decisions at the local level. Its focus is on the pollution control history of RK Excel Co., Ltd., a metal-plating industry operating in the Shiga Prefecture since 1951. The authors assess what motivates an individual company, such as RK Excel, to make the environmental decisions it does. Formal laws and regulations appear to have a less important role than community pressure in influencing industries to improve their environmental performance. Community pressure, within the context of changing environmental values throughout Japan and expanding markets for pollution control equipment, has been the motivation for RK Excel's decisions to reduce its effluent discharges into the environment.

Hexavalent chromium (Cr^{6+}), the main pollutant from RK Excel's metal-plating operations, has severe toxic and carcinogenic effects if released into the environment and ingested. RK Excel's by-products, such as reduced chromium (Cr^{3+}), copper, and nickel, are less toxic metals.

Although RK Excel has implemented various methods of effluent quality control since 1951, its basic processes have remained virtually unchanged: reduction of Cr^{6+} to Cr^{3+}, coagulation-sedimentation, and pH neutralization. What has changed over time are the extent and quality of these methods. Following is a chronological account of RK Excel's pollution control activities since 1951.

PHASE I: 1951–58. In the first phase no formal environmental regulations were in operation. The main purpose of the company's antipollution activities was to control the discharge of Cr^{6+}. RK Excel used simple earthen pits as reactors, and Cr^{6+} effluent was controlled effectively.

PHASE II: 1959–69. During the late 1950s, rice output declined in fields using water from a pond receiving inflows of RK Excel's effluent. Fish in the pond were also adversely affected.

In response, RK Excel took two important actions. First, in 1959, it introduced improved lime-dosing and pH neutralizing systems. Second, it compensated farmers for damages. These actions were done to maintain good relations with the community. Fear of being ostracized by the community was crucial in fostering improved environmental performance.

PHASE III: 1970–72. With the increase in the public's environmental consciousness in Japan in the 1960s, and with the new leadership of the country's "pro-environment" prime minister, K. Tanaka, RK Excel initiated a major upgrade of its pollution control processes in 1970. For example, it abandoned use of open pits, constructed coagulation-sedimentation tanks with improved pumps and meters, and further upgraded its pH neutralization system. Markets for pollution control equipment were rapidly developing. At the national level, the Water Pollution Control Law was enacted in 1970. RK Excel, however, did not attribute its decision to upgrade its processes to this legislation but rather to the growing public awareness of environmental issues.

PHASE IV: 1973 TO PRESENT. RK Excel implemented a fully automated pollution control system in 1973. (Most factories in Japan started automating in the early 1970s.) At the local level, stricter regulations were implemented under the 1972 Pollution Control Ordinance of Shiga. RK Excel, however, changed its processes to bring the company in line with general industry practice. Pollution control efforts were undertaken primarily to maintain the best practice at the time.

In 1976 RK Excel and the residents of Yagura town signed a pollution control agreement. In late March residents living one kilometer from the RK Excel factory complained of severe skin irritation for more than a year. They also noted that the color of water pumped from their wells had turned yellow, and they suspected that the well water was contaminated. Analysis showed that the water was contaminated with Cr^{6+}, at a concentration of 8.2 milligrams per liter. Contamination was, therefore, very high since the drinking water standard was 0.05 milligrams per liter.

This finding was immediately reported to the Pollution Control Department of the Shiga Prefecture Government. Following its own investigation at the factory, the Shiga Government established that the source of pollution was the leakage of hexavalent chromium from the concrete floor of a chrome-plating tank in the factory. Soil below the tank was also contaminated. The Shiga Government required the factory to (a) terminate its metal-plating processes; (b) replace the broken chrome-plating tank; (c) treat all the polluted soil within its compound; and (d) pump and treat groundwater from the contaminated wells. The treatment and monitoring of groundwater quality were to continue until the concentration of hexavalent chromium met the drinking water quality standard of 0.05 milligrams per liter. To date, RK Excel is still undertaking the pump-and-treat operation. Since 1977 it has cost RK Excel between 300 million and 400 million yen to treat and monitor groundwater quality.

RK Excel complied with the foregoing orders set by the Shiga Prefecture Government; it also did the following:

- Paid the cost of switching from groundwater to piped water for Kusatsu City residents whose well water had been contaminated.
- Covered the costs of medical examination and treatment of affected residents.
- Reached an out-of-court settlement with Yagura residents in mid-September 1976 by agreeing to pay a total of 34 million yen as compensation.

This case study highlights three key points. First, in controlling industrial pollution, community pressure is extremely important. Second, institutional and government capacity at the local level must be developed. Third, pollution prevention is easier and less costly to implement than pollution remediation.

Economic Incentives to Promote Compliance: Japan's Environmental Soft Loan Program

Compliance with and enforcement of environmental regulations are often hindered by a lack of economic resources or incentives. The case study by Akihisa Mori, Soo Cheol Lee, and Kazuhiro

Ueta (see Chapter 5) examines how one form of economic incentive, the environmental soft loan program, contributed to the overall system of environmental policies in Japan.

The case study focuses on (a) the incentive effects of environmental soft loans on firms' investments in pollution control equipment and (b) the preconditions for an environmental soft loan program that is effective. The program was created to reduce the cost to firms of complying with tighter environmental regulations. The Central Government mobilizes savings at low cost (for example, postal savings, national pension) and allocates the funds to public financial institutions for lending at preferential rates of interest. During the postwar reconstruction period, soft loan funds were used to finance strategic industries, such as electricity, steel, coal mining, and shipping. In the 1970s, when industrial pollution became a major public concern, the use of soft loans was expanded to include financing pollution abatement investments.

The major public financial institutions engaged in lending funds through the environmental soft loan program are the Japan Development Bank (JDB), the Japan Financial Corporation for Small Business (JFCSB), and the Japan Environment Corporation (JEC). Together these three institutions accounted for 95 percent of the total environmental soft loans disbursed in 1975. JDB provides environmental soft loans to big businesses, JFCSB and JEC to small and medium-sized enterprises (SMEs). The lending rate is usually set 1 percent to 2 percent lower than the long-term prime interest rate for big firms, and about 2 percent to 3 percent lower for SMEs. JDB and JFCSB generally set a lending rate higher than the borrowing rate; JEC sets the lending rate lower than the borrowing rate to reduce the investment cost for small and medium-size enterprises.

The "incentive" effect of the preferential interest rate applied over the repayment period of a soft loan can be estimated based on the amount of the firm's pollution abatement investment, the loan ratio caused by the soft loan, and the difference between the open market rate prevailing during a particular time period (month) and the preferential interest rate. Specifically, the effect of the preferential interest rate of a soft loan can be calculated in every time period—from the time of the loan until its repayment—and then added up by fiscal year. In the case of JDB, analysis has shown that the overall effect throughout the 1965–95 period was "negative" (–3.78 billion yen). This suggests that soft loans did not always provide a subsidy to firms during the period analyzed. (A "negative" effect means a financial cost burden to firms.) The "positive" (subsidy) effect of the preferential interest rate during the 1960s and 1970s, for example, was more than offset by the "negative" effect experienced for most of the 1980s and 1990s when the open market rate declined considerably. In the case of JEC, the overall effect was "positive" (83.57 billion yen). This is because JEC's lending rate was always lower than JDB's over the loan period analyzed.

Regression analysis based on a logarithmic function was used to estimate the "incentive" effect of soft loans on large firms' investment decisions concerning pollution abatement technologies. The total amount of investments for pollution control facilities undertaken by big firms during 1968 through 1993 was a function of (a) the size of the soft loan, (b) the preferential interest rate, and (c) tax savings from special tax breaks for pollution control investments. The analysis showed that the size of the soft loan (significant at the 1 percent level) provided the strongest incentive for firms to undertake pollution abatement investments. The preferential interest rate is significant at the 5 percent level, while the tax savings factor is not significant.

Four important factors contributed to the success of the environmental soft loan program in Japan. The first was the timing of the soft loan package, which was put together when the government established tight pollution standards. The package provided industries with considerable assistance in responding quickly to these regulations. In support of this package an information sharing system for government and business was set up. The pollution abatement investment needs of firms was matched with available soft loan funds from public banks. MITI collected information on demand for pollution abatement investments through JDB and other public financial institutions, and it relayed this information to the government.

Second, investment loans for designated "standard"' pollution abatement technology were provided to firms, regardless of their environmental performance. Performance evaluations by MITI had to show that the standard technologies would result in significant reductions in pollution. This second factor promoted the development of an environmental abatement technology industry in Japan. The demand for a pollution abatement technology naturally increased once it was designated as "standard" and a soft loan could be provided for firms to invest in it.

Third, public financial institutions did not conduct ex-post monitoring of the actual reductions in pollution. Instead, monitoring was carried out by the local government, which also strictly enforced environmental regulations. Firms that did not comply with regulations could be ordered to close down production or to relocate. At the same time, there existed a "partnership" between JEC and the local government that directly influenced a firm's behavior. Firms applying for a soft loan from JEC could only do so with the prior approval of the local government, stating that the technology investment was needed. Strict regulatory enforcement by the local government ensured that firms did not divert funds to other uses.

Lastly, Japan's environmental soft loan program was financed through the Fiscal Investment and Loan Program. Public banks were charged a fixed interest rate on their borrowings and given a repayment period of fifteen years. They were allowed to vary their annual borrowings according to demand for soft loan funds, and they could set the interest charges for those funds. The repayment period for loaned out funds was five to twenty years, and this enabled public banks to use repaid loans as a revolving fund. Thus, banks were able to conduct business for a profit, and firms were able to comply with environmental regulations without delay.

The Link between Compliance at the Local Level and Global Environmental Goals: Waste Reduction Measures in Nagoya City

The case study by Kazuhiro Ueta (see Chapter 6) investigates the possible effects of local environmental actions on global environmental issues. For example, it explores how the waste reduction measures taken by Nagoya City could have affected global warming. The case study also analyzes the cost-effectiveness of implementing measures for waste reduction and recycling given the difficulties in finding suitable sites for final waste disposal.

Although costs for addressing issues such as global warming are to be covered by each local community, it is hard for these communities to directly realize the resulting benefits. At the same time, measures taken for local communities, such as antipollution policies, are often implemented without acknowledging their impact on global environmental conservation. In fact, measures taken to conserve the global environment often improve the quality of the local environment, and measures taken for the local environment often contribute to global environmental conservation. This "synergy effect" must be taken into account in the decision-making process. An awareness is needed of the ancillary benefits from promoting environmental conservation and efficient environmental control. Measures to mitigate global warming, measures that tend to be viewed as irrelevant by the local community, must be linked to its specific needs.

Benefits from the synergy effect can be classified in three ways: (1) benefits to other fields from measures to mitigate global warming; (2) benefits to global warming mitigation from efforts in other fields, such as antipollution measures; and (3) aggregate benefits of the measures to mitigate global warming and to address other environmental problems. The first two types of benefits are called ancillary benefits; benefits in the third category are called co-benefits.

In 1996 Nagoya City generated about one million tons of solid wastes. Nearly 70 percent was domestic wastes (such as kitchen refuse, plastic containers, packaging materials, etc.). The city constructed a disposal site in Tajimi, Gifu Prefecture, but its landfill capacity became very limited. Plans were developed to construct another landfill in the Fujimae tidal flat. Since this tidal flat was a habitat for migratory birds, the plans met strong opposition from the public and were eventually abandoned.

In 1999, alarmed by the critical need to deal with huge urban wastes and the lack of adequate disposal sites due to physical and social land use constraints, Nagoya City declared a state of emergency. An action plan for waste disposal was formulated. The goal was to reduce wastes by 200,000 tons (20 percent) over two years, with participation from the local residents. Various specific measures were implemented. Collection of cans and bottles was extended to cover all the sixteen wards in the city. Voluntary collection of wastes by citizens was promoted through subsidy provisions. In addition, recycling of solid wastes and incineration efficiency were improved. Several Japanese cities, including Nagoya, have depended upon waste incineration, although it has been associated with significant local energy costs and CO_2 emissions contributing to the problem of global warming.

By 2000, two years after the declaration of the state of emergency, Nagoya City had significantly improved its waste disposal through implementation of its waste reduction and recycling program. The following achievements are noteworthy:

- The disposal of combustible wastes decreased by 20 percent in 2000. Partly because of strict controls on separated collections, wastes formerly disposed as combustible wastes were collected as recyclable wastes.
- The amount of recyclable wastes collected by the city tripled.
- Final waste disposal, including incineration, decreased by half.

Thus, Nagoya City succeeded in achieving a large-scale reduction in wastes disposal through measures implemented after the declaration of the state of emergency.

The case study quantifies the changes in CO_2 emissions associated with the above-mentioned results. Key findings are as follows:

- CO_2 emissions during the process of waste collection increased in 2000 by about 1,500 tons.
- As Nagoya City significantly reduced its amount of wastes for incineration, CO_2 emissions during the incineration process decreased in 2000 by 60,000 tons.
- For the whole waste disposal process, CO_2 emissions were reduced by 55,000 tons in 2000.

The case study also analyzed the cost-effectiveness of Nagoya City's waste reduction/recycling measures, and their contribution to global warming mitigation. Important results of the analysis are as follows:

- Nagoya City's waste disposal reduction measures were driven by the problems it encountered in securing a final waste disposal site. The benefit of postponing construction of a disposal site, through waste reduction measures, was estimated at 6.25 billion yen.
- The total amount of waste disposal decreased by 20 percent (or 198,463 tons) in 2000, while the costs of waste disposal increased by 4 billion yen. Meanwhile, the reduction in the amount of disposed wastes (for example, because of recycling) resulted in CO_2 emissions abatement of 55,000 tons. Using the carbon tax of 3,000 yen per ton of CO_2, the authors estimate the benefit of CO_2 abatement to be 165 million yen.
- The benefit/cost ratio was estimated at 1.56: the benefit of postponing construction of a disposal site (6.25 billion yen) was evaluated against the costs required for waste reduction measures (4 billion yen). The benefit/cost ratio increased to 1.60 when the benefits of reducing CO_2 emissions were taken into account.

Based on the above analysis, Nagoya City's waste reduction measures were cost-effective. Although they were measures implemented to deal with local pollution problems, they contributed to global warming mitigation.

Most developing countries do not use incineration, and they view the employment associated with disposal sites as an economic benefit. Thus, this example from Nagoya City is not directly applicable to the situation of most developing countries. However, other local environmental concerns could be linked to clean air, and habitat issues could be relevant to global environmental programs. If there are joint local and global benefits, the framework used in Nagoya could help in the process of evaluating these benefits. Indeed, global environmental financing might be incorporated in local strategies for environmental management.

A Comparison of Japan and East Asian Developing Countries

Japan's rapid industrial growth during the postwar period resembles in some ways the growth during the 1990s in many developing countries in East Asia. The timing of development is different, however, and so are the sources of pollution, particularly air pollution.

Sources of Pollution

In many developing countries in East Asia, including Indonesia, Thailand, and the Philippines, widespread air pollution in cities is caused mainly by motor vehicles. In contrast, during Japan's early industrialization phase, the main concern was to control air pollution caused by coal and heavy oil use in power and industrial development and in home and building heating.

In Vietnam environmental pollution was not placed high on the country's agenda until the early 1990s, following passage of the Law on Environmental Protection and the establishment of the Ministry of Science, Technology and Environment (MOSTE) in 1993.[1] In Japan attention to urban air pollution problems began much earlier. Citizens' anti-pollution movements began before in the 1960s, and growing environmental awareness among local residents and the mass media in the 1970s forced governments at the national and local levels to establish pollution control measures in Japan (see Table 1.1) and set up ambient environmental quality standards. The industry, transportation, and construction sectors are the significant sources of air pollution in Vietnam. Old factories (built before 1975) and small and medium-scale industries with old production technologies are the major emitters of air pollutants in that country. Very few of these facilities have scrubber equipment. Most of the old industries ended up within the confines of urban centers. For example, Ho Chi Minh City has about 700 factories; 500 of them are located in the urban areas. In Hanoi 200 out of 300 factories are located in the urban areas.

Japan and Vietnam also differ in terms of pollutant sources. Factory emissions in many Japanese cities during the early industrialization phase caused alarm. In contrast, the two worst sources of air pollution in Vietnam are: (a) dust from industrial production and construction activities and (b) emissions from mobile sources. Monitoring results for 1995 to 2001 indicate that dust concentrations in residential areas close to factories or near major roads were often two or three times higher than the permitted levels. The places with the highest levels of dust pollution were residential areas near Hai Phong cement plant, VICASA plant in Bien Hoa Province, Tan Binh industrial zone in Ho Chi Minh City, and Hon Gai coal plant in Ha Long City.

Construction activities throughout Vietnam, particularly in the urban centers, have generated serious dust pollution problems. Monitoring results for the 1995-2001 period show that 60 percent to 70 percent of dust volume in urban air is from construction activities.

Pollution in Vietnam is caused by mobile sources as well as by urban and industrial expansion. The number of motor vehicles has increased sharply in Vietnam's major cities. Before the 1980s, 80 percent to 90 percent of urban residents used bicycles. Today 80 percent of these residents are using motorcycles. The number of registered motorcycles in Vietnam has increased at an annual rate of between 15 percent and 18 percent. Vehicle emissions are particularly troublesome in large cities such as Hanoi, Ho Chi Minh City, Hai Phong, and Da Nang.

The Political Context for Environmental Compliance and Enforcement

A major obstacle to effective environmental compliance and enforcement in East Asia is the lack of political support for the environment. For example, in Indonesia there is little or no political support for environmental management.[2] This is very different from the experience of Japan, a country where political will has been critically important in addressing pollution concerns. Citizens' protests against pollution and fear of being voted out of office in favor of leftist politicians have motivated incumbent local officials to enforce stringent emission reduction targets. In Indonesia political will was inadequate at the time when industrial development programs were being implemented, and environmental pollution was not an important issue in the mind of the general public.

Lack of political support for environmental measures is accompanied by poor interagency coordination. In Indonesia the Ministry of the Environment has the major task of coordinating environmental activities in the provinces. Nonetheless, the environmental decision making has not been fully transparent across relevant government agencies, and often it lacks the participation of stakeholders.

Integration of environmental regulations with sectoral department policies also proved extremely difficult to implement in Indonesia. Forestry, mining, fishery, agriculture, and industry are sectors associated with strong economic interests, and they implement programs without coordination among themselves or with national ministries and local official agencies. Regulatory enforcement and compliance remain at the margins.

In the case of Thailand, the potential for interagency coordination has been undermined by some agencies' failure to abide by agreements.[3] In some cases consensus has been achieved, but some parties have not fully cooperated in carrying out the agreed actions.

Sometimes the problem of a lack of consensus extends beyond government agencies. Communities may be at odds with private companies over pollution-related issues. Indeed, some communities have demonstrated to demand cancellation of projects. In the late 1990s, the Thai government decided to postpone the construction of two coal-fired power plants for two years because of community demands. This has been repeated in many instances throughout East Asia.

The Role of Local Governments in Environmental Management

Japan has a long history of local environmental management, and local governments have the authority and capability to establish and enforce environmental laws. These are factors that have contributed significantly to the control of urban air pollution in Japan. In contrast, in Indonesia major development decisions are made at the central government level. Traditionally, local governments have had little opportunity to make development plans based on local potential and local needs. Then, in the late 1990s, the political system in Indonesia was transformed from a centralized to a decentralized form of government, and environmental laws provided for a stronger role for local governments. Based on the environmental law enacted in 1997, the local governments were granted authority to carry out their own environmental management plans.

The lack of local government authority is not the only constraint on environmental compliance and enforcement in developing countries in East Asia. Often the role and involvement of local government are quite limited by budgets, personnel, and technical capability. Environmental management potential, especially at the local level, also differs markedly in Japan and in developing countries. For example, in Vietnam, following the establishment of the environmental inspection service in 1994, 60 out of 61 provinces in the country had an environmental inspection division under the Department of Science, Technology, and Environment (DOSTE). However, these inspection divisions are so understaffed that it is difficult for them to monitor compliance with environmental regulations. Consequently, most environmental violations have been reported by residents who live close to factories instead of by the inspection service.

In Thailand the Constitution of 1997 delegated to local governments administrative and management authority that had been held by the national government. However, lack of trained personnel and technical capability at the local level remain obstacles to effective implementation of environmental measures.

In Indonesia the process of devolving power from the central government to local governments is even more recent. Act No. 22/1999 now enables local governments to formulate their own development plan with input from the local population. In addition, Act No. 25/1999 on Fiscal Balance provides local governments and communities with financial resources and authority to manage their own natural resources for economic development. However, there is still a need to develop the technical and financial capacity at the local government level.

The lack of professional and technical expertise at the local government level is a common constraint in developing countries. In Japan environmental professionals are given high status, and it is not difficult to attract them into local government service. In contrast, in Thailand, as in many other developing countries, environmental engineers have yet to be given high status in government and their wages in government agencies remain low. Thus, there are few government officials knowledgeable about pollution control and management, and this has had a debilitating impact on the country's ability to address its environmental problems.

Economic Incentives

Soft loan programs can help developing countries achieve pollution reductions at reduced costs.[4] However, certain conditions must be met before an environmental soft loan program can be implemented successfully. In Japan large sums are available for environmental soft loans from domestic sources, such as postal savings and pension funds. In developing countries the funding for environmental incentive programs often comes from foreign sources. For example, in Indonesia funding has come from financial institutions like JBIC (Japan Bank for International Cooperation) and KfW (an international aid agency in Germany).

Major public financial institutions are engaged in the execution of Japan's environmental soft loan programs. JDB lends to big businesses; JFCSB and JEC extend soft loans largely to small and medium-size enterprises. In contrast, Indonesia has a less-organized and focused system for executing its environmental soft loan programs. The Central Bank asks banks to distribute soft loans when funds become available from abroad, or, in the case of environmental loan funds from KfW, provincial development banks and commercial banks are appointed as executing institutions.

In Indonesia, unlike in Japan there is no specialized network of financial institutions to implement the economic incentives programs. Another difference in the use of economic incentives has a longer term implication: in Japan, soft loans are intended to cover only the capital expenditures of pollution abatement investments; in Indonesia, soft loan programs also cover operation and maintenance costs. In developing countries, environmental training of industry personnel is important to build capacities for dealing with environmental concerns.

In the case of China, economic incentives have been increasingly used to promote environmental management and compliance.[5] The "polluter pays" principle has been incorporated in the design of the economic incentive system in China. Pilot projects in Tianjin and Shenyang, China, are using pollution charges as revolving funds to help in pollution management. In Japan, however, the soft loan program was not built upon the "polluter pays" principle, and this shortcoming has increased the possibility of low efficiency in the implementation of the program.

China, Indonesia, and other developing countries may have an advantage over Japan in another area: their emphasis on "clean production technologies" rather than "end-of-pipe technologies" to reduce pollution. In the early days developing countries did stress end-of-pipe technologies because these technologies satisfied the needs of the time; developing "clean production technologies" would have taken too long for the government to respond to social demands for a cleaner environment. From the viewpoint of developing countries today, investments in "clean production technologies" are more favored than "end-of-pipe technologies."

Implementing Environmental Management: Conditions for Success

Effective monitoring is one of the most important conditions for ensuring a successful environmental management program. In Japan local governments have been very effective in monitoring to determine if industries are in compliance with the local environmental regulations. Local governments also are involved in approving soft loan proposals by evaluating if the investment is needed. In many developing countries, however, environmental accountability is still at the discussion stage. Without accountability, monitoring of pollution control and industries' compliance with regulations would be difficult to implement.

Strict enforcement of environmental regulations by the local and national governments and strong public support for a clean environment are important reasons for Japan's achievement of substantive improvements in environmental quality. In many developing countries, however, the opposite actually holds. There is a lack of public awareness of environmental issues, and regulatory enforcement mechanisms are weak—factors that impede a country's ability to implement economic incentives, such as soft loan programs. For gains in environmental quality, monitoring capacities and regulatory enforcement at the local levels of government need to be greatly improved, local citizens' participation in environmental management must be promoted, and accountability needs to be incorporated in the system.

Many of the successful environmental management efforts in Japan directly involve the participation of local government, industry, and the community in investigating the pollution problem, deciding on environmental standards, and implementing remedial actions. These experiences are relevant to similar initiatives that can be observed in developing countries in East Asia.

The Japanese experience has demonstrated that good governance is central to achieving a clean, healthy environment. In Indonesia the Ministry of Environment has introduced a "Good Environmental Governance Program" to strengthen local government capacities to enforce environmental regulations and encourage the active participation of local residents.

Japan's overall approach to promoting compliance with environmental standards has been based on the concept of "deterrence" or "command and control." The effectiveness of this approach depends on the motivation of industries to comply and on public environmental awareness and the willingness of people to cooperate to find a solution to environmental problems. In Indonesia the Environmental Management Act of 1997 (EMA 1997) is also based on the "deterrence" approach. This legislation includes provisions for soft loans to assist industries in undertaking pollution abatement investments.

In Indonesia, like in Japan, public pressure has proved to be an effective instrument to settle environmental disputes. Consider the case of the pulp and paper factory located in northern Sumatra. A few years ago local residents complained that the factory had polluted rivers and caused deforestation. They also complained about the foul odor coming from the factory. Public demands and pressure by nongovernmental organizations forced the local government to order the factory to close down.

Indonesia's experience with groundwater pollution also demonstrates some similarities to the Japanese experience in terms of local involvement.[6] Groundwater in West Java was contaminated when gasoline was accidentally spilled during the filling of a ground tank in a gasoline station in Bogor. In an experience similar to the one described earlier in the case study on RK Excel, the local community received compensation payments from the gasoline industry. Unlike RK Excel, however, the industry was not required by law to undertake clean-up measures. The case study of RK

Excel underlines the importance of monitoring, a quick response system, and technology adoption in pollution control.

In the Philippines, community awareness and initiatives in Cebu Province helped the local government control toxic contamination.[7] The toxic contamination incident was brought to the attention of government agencies, local officials, the local business community, and the mass media. The polluting company was forced to comply with environmental regulations and treat its chromium discharge because of pressures from the government and community as a whole. In the Philippine system, because local governments have limited authority to enforce environmental laws, the media and community organizations play a key role in pressuring polluting companies to comply with legislative regulations.

The pollution problem was similar to the case in the Shiga Prefecture of pollution by a metal-plating industry. Cebu Province also experienced toxic contamination of groundwater involving hexavalent chromium caused by a metal plating industry. In the Cebu case, however, the provincial water company discovered the toxic pollution of one of its production wells while the degree of pollution was still relatively early. Thus, the water quality with respect to hexavalent chromium was restored to meet the standard (0.05 mg/l) within a year.

In Thailand experience with developing pollution standards has shown that national regulations tend to be too general and that local criteria are needed. Thailand's first and largest petrochemical complex is located in the Map Ta Pud District of Rayong Province in the eastern seaboard. The air pollution problem from this complex is similar to the air pollution problem that occurred in 1955 in Yokkaichi City.

When the factories in the petrochemical complex in Thailand started operating fully around 1997, a community downwind from the complex began complaining about the offensive odor of various volatile organic compounds (VOCs). Schoolchildren in the community school located less than 1 kilometer from the petrochemical complex suffered respiratory illnesses. Six major factories, including two refineries, were identified as sources of VOCs emissions. As in the case of Kitakyushu City of Fukuoka in 1970, a joint committee consisting of representatives from national and local government agencies, industries, and the community was established to develop air pollution control measures and then monitor their implementation. After more than two years the offensive odor had been reduced more than 90 percent.

There is currently a plan to establish in the Map Ta Pud area a new coal-fired power plant on land reclaimed from the sea. Local communities are concerned that air pollution will increase again. A comprehensive study is being undertaken to determine whether the area can assimilate such a plant and whether further industrial development is feasible without causing adverse impacts on air quality in the vicinity. The study will also establish the fair distribution of financial and operational burdens to be shared among factories according to their contribution to the air pollution. This case is similar to that of Kitakyushu City.

With regard to local initiatives, the situation in Vietnam has some similarities to Japanese experience (in particular, to the key role of local involvement in achieving successful pollution control in Osaka City). Vietnam, unlike other developing-country cases noted earlier, has seen traditional cooperation between local governments, local residents, and local businesses. Vietnam attaches importance to this kind of cooperation in dealing successfully with pollution problems caused by the Phailai thermal power plant. The plant, a state-owned enterprise, was established in 1960 to supply electricity to eight provinces in the Red River Delta. Its facilities were outdated and inefficient. Although the plant was causing serious air pollution in the area, it continued to operate in order to meet the growing demand for electricity. Citizens' complaints about plant emissions became more frequent and vocal during the mid-1990s. As a result of public pressure, the Department of Science, Technology and the Environment and the National Environment Agency (NEA) decided to implement environmental improvements in the power plant's operations.

In response to citizens' protests, NEA conducted plant inspections, collected data on the environmental and health consequences of plant emissions, and involved local residents, power sector personnel, government officials, and the mass media in a "participatory approach" to reaching a solution. Through these efforts, power plant officials agreed to (a) comply with the Law on Environmental Protection; (b) invest 12 billion Vietnam dollars (VND) in new dust precipitators; and (c) pay 900 million VND to affected residents. In this instance in Vietnam, as in Osaka City, effective pollution control was achieved as a result of several factors—public pressure, the political will to enforce regulations, and the commitment of industry to comply with environmental regulations.

Conclusion

Despite increasing recognition of the ill effects of pollution and the enactment of various environmental management laws and regulations, pollution monitoring and compliance in developing countries in East Asia continue to lag. One of the main constraints to practical implementation of pollution control is the lack of environmental awareness and sustained public involvement at the local level. The experience of Japan, where communities became active proponents of pollution control and local governments and industries were pressed to adopt pollution abatement activities, is of relevance to developing countries today. The case studies from Japan and the reviews of developing-country resource persons indicate that some Japanese approaches may not be directly transferable to developing countries. However, the wide range of approaches to promote cooperation among community organizations, local government agencies, and concerned industries in Japan's experience provide useful models that may be adapted to conditions in developing countries.

Notes

1. The discussion of issues regarding Vietnam is based on the review by Nam Thang Do (see Appendix A).
2. Examples for Indonesia are based on the review by Rosa Vivien Ratnawati (see Appendix A).
3. Examples from Thailand are based on the review by Supat Wangwongwatana (see Appendix A).
4. The relevance of the soft loan program to Indonesia was reviewed by Budi Widianarko (see Appendix A).
5. The examples for China are based on the review by Jianyu Zhang (see Appendix A).
6. Water pollution issues in Indonesia are based on the review by Indra Mufardi Roesli (see Appendix A).
7. The Philippine examples are based on the review by Ruben Almendras (see Appendix A).

2

Successful Air Pollution Control in Japan: History and Implications

Ryo Fujikura

Japan succeeded in achieving rapid economic development in the 1960s by promoting heavy industries. Because this industrial expansion was attained without sound consideration of environmental consequences, industrial cities in Japan experienced serious pollution. As a result, the country's industrial policy during the late 1960s and the early 1970s drastically shifted from a focus on "economic development" to "pollution control." Since then the urban environment in Japan has steadily improved to an acceptable level. This improvement in environmental quality is known as "Japan's Pollution Miracle" (Broadbent 1998, 18-20). Table 2.1 shows the timeline and scope of the evolution of pollution regulation in Japan.

This chapter identifies the social and economic context in which this "miracle" occurred. It tries to clarify why Japanese industry so intensively invested in air pollution control measures, actions that can lower not only a company's profit but also its productivity. Focusing on air pollution from stationary sources, particularly on dust fall and sulfur oxide pollution, the chapter presents (1) the history of Japan's response at the national level to the problem of air pollution, including the constraints encountered in implementation of pollution control measures and the factors that contributed to Japan's eventual successes in compliance and enforcement; and (2) detailed examples of envirionmental management efforts in four cities.

Part I. Air Pollution in Japan and Factors Affecting Environmental Management

Prewar Period

By the late nineteenth century, air in some Japanese industrial cities was already polluted (mainly by coal dust). In response to increasing complaints from local residents, the Osaka Prefecture Government prohibited the establishment of factories emitting significant amounts of soot in downtown areas; specifically, it enacted in 1931 the "Osaka Regulation for Soot and Smoke Prevention." (Please refer to Table 2.1.) The purpose of this law was to regulate soot according to the Lingerman Chart, which measures the intensity of smoke. Then the prefecture government and the Osaka Municipal Government encouraged factories to use relevant technologies to improve their combustion efficiency. Despite these efforts, urban air pollution problems were not solved, and Osaka became notorious as the "City of Smoke."

This chapter is based on interviews with former local and national government officials, former employees of local industries, and local citizens. The author expresses special thanks to Katsumi Saruta (former director of the Pollution Control Bureau, Yokohama Municipal Government); Satoshi Nakazono, director of the Environment Conservation Department, Kitakyushu Municipal Government; and Takshi Matsumiya (former director of Environment Department, Osaka Municipal Government). The author also would like to express his sincere gratitude to Michio Hashimoto (former director of Pollution Control of the Ministry of Health and former director general of the Air Pollution Quality Bureau of the Environment Agency) for his kind review of an earlier draft and his useful suggestions.

Table 2.1 *Timeline and Scope of Japan's Key Pollution Control Regulations*

Time period and scope	Pollution control measure	Key developments
Prewar period		
Late 19th century, Osaka	Osaka Prefectural Orders	Issued in response to increasing complaints from the public; prohibited factories that would emit a significant amount of soot from locating in downtown areas.
1931, Osaka	Osaka Regulation for Soot and Smoke Prevention	Established to regulate soot emissions. Factories were also required to adopt new technologies to improve combustion efficiencies. Nonetheless, air pollution persisted, and Osaka became known as the "City of Smoke."
Postwar period		
1949, Tokyo Metropolitan	Tokyo Ordinance for Factory Pollution Control	Issued in response to growing public complaints about air pollution. Because the ordinance did not explicitly define the technical criteria for pollution control, it was not effective.
1951, Ube	Resolution (adopted by an ad hoc committee at municipal level) for dust fall control	Required local industries to install precipitators to control dust emissions. Although initially poor, compliance by industries had improved significantly by 1953.
1955, Fukuoka	Fukuoka Ordinance for Pollution Control	Stipulated technical criteria for pollution control. Lack of appropriate antipollution technologies hindered implementation. Enforcement was weak partly because of strong opposition from local businesses.
1955, Japan	Bill for Standards on Living Environmental Pollution Control	Drafted by the Ministry of Health in response to the damaging effects of air pollution on local residents. Strong business sector opposition blocked the introduction of the bill to the Diet.
Energy shift period		
1960s, Japan	Economic factors rather than regulations were the reason for significant reductions in coal dust fall in major industrial cities in Japan in the 1960s.	Industries throughout Japan switched from domestic coal to imported heavy oil, and sulfur oxides replaced coal dusts as the main source of air pollution. Strikes by coal mine workers had increased the price of coal and destabilized supply. The development of oil fields in the Middle East made imported oil more competitive than Japanese coal.
1962, Japan	Soot and Smoke Control Law	Established as a result of collaboration between the Ministry of Health and MITI. The sulfur oxides emission standards were not realistic to control pollution levels, and they were applied to certain designated areas only. Enforcement was delegated only to the municipal government and did not include the prefectural level. Desulfurization technologies had not yet been developed. Because of its serious limitations, the law was not effective.
1967, Japan	Basic Law for Pollution Control	Established by the national government. This law, like the Soot and Smoke Control Law, stipulated "undertaking living environmental management in harmony

(Table continues on the following page.)

Table 2.1 *(continued)*

Time period and scope	Pollution control measure	Result
		with sound industrial development." Businesses succeeded in weakening pollution control activities. Although the Basic Law for Pollution Control did not directly improve the urban environment in Japan, it included measures that later helped control air pollution in cities. The law established the ambient environmental quality standards (EQSs) for sulfur oxides.
1968, Japan	Air Pollution Control Law	Replaced the Soot and Smoke Control Law (1962); regulated sulfur oxides emissions from factories and nitrogen oxides from automobiles. The law became the fundamental tool for achieving the EQSs established in succeeding years.
1970s, Japan	Pollution Control Diet Session was convened by Prime Minister E. Sato; 14 environmental conservation bills were passed.	Established the Environment Agency. Deleted from the Basic Law for Pollution Control the controversial provision on harmonization of living environmental management with sound industrial development. In Yokohama, Tokyo, Kawasaki, and other cities, citizens replaced Liberal Democratic Party incumbents with members of the Socialist Party. The Socialist Party was believed to enforce more stringent pollution control measures.

Source: Unpublished documents of the Ministry of the Environment of Japan and interviews of national and city officials undertaken by the case study author.

During the prewar period, air pollution in the Tokyo metropolitan area was a serious problem as well. Between 1924 and 1936 the Tokyo Metropolitan Police received 246 petitions and complaints; of these, 46 were for soot and 25 were for dust fall (IPCS 1970). Dust fall in Tokyo's downtown areas reached 18 tons per square kilometer per month in 1927, indicating that domestic use of coal for heating was a significant pollution source (Hishida 1974). Local residents continuously petitioned the local governments to take appropriate measures, but air quality only got worse.

By contrast, in Kitakyushu City, local citizens appeared to welcome signs of air pollution. Residents of the Yahata Area, which later became a part of Kitakyushu, noted (in a 1909 essay) that "sparrows in Yahata are black." Sparrows in Japan are typically brown, but darker sparrows might have become dominant in this area at the beginning of the twentieth century (Yahata Works 1980). Although no scientific investigation was conducted, the thick black smoke being emitted from the 136 chimneys in Yahata may have made brown sparrows black. Black smoke was regarded by the local citizens as a symbol of successful modernization.[1]

Postwar Period

World War II was over in the Asian theater on August 15, 1945. Japan's physical infrastructure was completely destroyed. After the war tens of thousands of Japanese people returned home from northeastern China and the Korean Peninsula. Japan had to reconstruct its economy to feed its people. Until the early 1950s, finding food and meeting other necessities of daily life were the main concerns of the Japanese people. However, local governments in major cities did receive complaints from citizens about pollution (for example, about offensive odor and dust). With the postwar reconstruction of industry and Japan's increasing population, pollution problems became more and more obvious.

INEFFECTIVE MEASURES BY THE TOKYO METROPOLITAN GOVERNMENT AND THE FUKUOKA PREFECTURE GOVERNMENT. In response to increasing complaints from the public, the Tokyo Metropolitan Government in 1949 established the Tokyo Ordinance for Factory Pollution Control. Because it failed to specify the technical criteria of "pollution" and simply prohibited "significant" pollution without precisely defining "significant," the ordinance was ineffective.

In 1955 the Fukuoka Prefecture Government established the Fukuoka Ordinance for Pollution Control despite strong opposition from local businesses, which feared pollution control measures would hinder economic development of the region (Shoji and Miyamoto 1964). This ordinance stipulated technical criteria for designating pollution but was not enforced. Even if more of an effort had been made to enforce this ordinance, it still would have been very difficult for the government to control pollution because of the lack of appropriate antipollution technologies at that time.

EFFECTIVE MEASURES IN UBE CITY. The major industries in Ube City, Yamaguchi Prefecture, were coal mining and cement production. Coal mined from Ube contained 40 percent to 45 percent ash, and the coal was used mostly for power generation. Coal and cement dust fall began to bother local residents in the late 1940s. By 1951 dust fall was recorded at 55.86 tons per square kilometer per month, the highest level for the world's 43 major cities where dust fall was being measured at that time (Nose 1997).

An ad hoc committee of the municipal assembly in Ube City adopted a resolution in 1951 to control dust fall. The resolution, which required every local factory to install a precipitator, was not taken seriously by local businesses. The municipal government entrusted a university professor with monitoring responsibilities, but monitoring was often obstructed and monitoring equipment even destroyed.

In 1953 a vice-president of Ube Kosan Company, a leading cement manufacturing company, visited Europe and the United Sates and became convinced of the importance of dust fall control. Subsequently, local factories undertook pollution control measures. Cement industries recognized that pollution control would not only improve air quality, but also would contribute to their economic profits. In fact, collecting and recycling cement dust improved their productivity. As a result, the number of precipitators installed in Ube City increased considerably after 1957, and recorded dust fall significantly decreased in the early 1960s as shown in Figure 2.1 (Ube City 1997). Unfortunately, this early experience in pollution control was not replicated in other Japanese industrial cities seriously affected by dust fall.

Energy Shift Period

Economic factors, more than governmental regulations for pollution control, reduced the problem of coal dust fall in Japan's major industrial cities. In the 1960s, industries throughout Japan changed their major energy source. Although the national government instituted measures to encourage Japan's industries to continue using domestic coal, they failed to comply. With the development of Middle Eastern oil fields, the price of foreign oil became cheaper than coal. The standard price of type C-heavy oil dropped by 50 percent from 1956 to 1969. The price of domestic coal was 7,400 yen per ton in 1969; the prices of one-kiloliter of A-, B-, and C-heavy oil were 10,000 yen, 7,000 yen, and 6,300 yen, respectively. The energy generated by one kiloliter of heavy oil was greater than that of one-ton coal (IPCS 1970). Moreover, the supply of domestic coal was unstable due to frequent coal mine strikes.

Oil had other advantages that made it the preferred fuel: oil was easier to handle, and required less storage space than coal. As factories switched from coal to oil, significant reductions in dust

Figure 2.1 *Dust Fall and Number of Precipitators in Ube City*

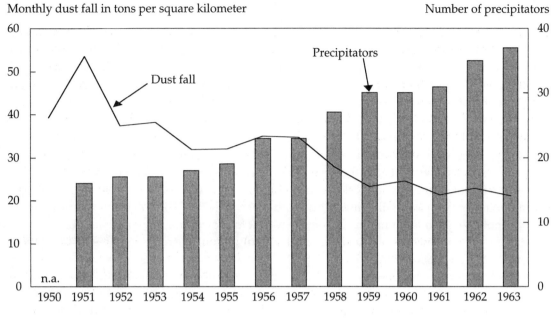

Source: Ube City (1997).

fall were observed throughout Japan. Figure 2.2 illustrates the correlation between the decline in the consumption of solid fuel (coal) and the decrease in the amount of dust fall in Shiroyama district of Kitakyushu City (Fujikura 1998).

Figure 2.2 *Solid Fuel Consumption and Dust Fall in Kitakyushu City*

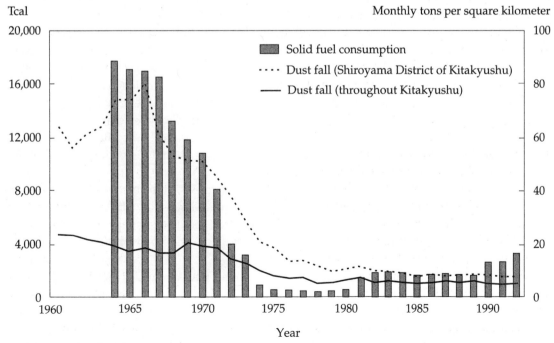

Source: Fujikura (1998).

INITIAL RESPONSE OF THE NATIONAL GOVERNMENT. As industries shifted from coal to heavy oil (which has a high sulfur content), and as energy consumption rapidly increased with industrialization, sulfur oxides replaced coal dust as the major air pollutant in Japan. Although the public was concerned about the adverse effects of pollution on human health, no consensus about pollution control emerged in Japanese society. In 1955 the Ministry of Health (MHW) had drafted the "Bill for Standards on Living Environmental Pollution Control," but it was not submitted to the Diet because of strong opposition from the business community. When air pollution worsened in the 1960s, the Ministry of International Trade and Industry (MITI) became openly concerned. It feared that extreme pollution and intensifying citizens' protests against pollution could hinder industrial development and economic growth. In 1962 the national government, in collaboration with the MHW and MITI, enacted the "Soot and Smoke Control Law."

Article 1 of this law stipulated the need "to undertake living environmental management in harmony with sound industrial development." This language reflected industries' claim that stringent air pollution controls would hinder their production activities. The authority to implement the law was not delegated to municipal governments but to prefectural governments, and emission standards were applied only within designated "pollution control areas." As a result, regulations were not enforced outside of these areas.

For a variety of reasons, setting stringent standards was not regarded as "realistic." Scientific knowledge about air pollution was still very limited, and desulfurization technologies had not yet been developed. In particular, during the "energy shift" period in the 1960s (see Table 1.1), the emission standard for sulfur oxides (sulfur dioxide and sulfuric anhydride) was set at 2,200 parts per million (ppm). Industries could easily meet this standard without undertaking additional pollution control measures; all that industries had to do was to continue using crude oil from the Middle East, which contained 3.5 percent sulfur. At that time Japanese industries were, in fact, heavily dependent on this crude oil. Moreover, power plants, the largest contributor to air pollution, were not subject to the law. Therefore, legal enforcement, particularly for prevention of air pollution, could not be expected.

WORSENING POLLUTION AND CITIZENS' RESPONSE. "The Income Doubling Plan," the economic plan adopted by the Japanese Cabinet in 1960, succeeded in expanding Japan's per capita gross national product (GNP) from US$4,706 to US$11,579 (in 1987 prices) during the 1960s (World Bank 1995). This increase was achieved through Japan's strong promotion of heavy industries. As a result of this promotion, crude steel production, for example, increased from 22.1 million tons in 1960 to 93.3 million tons in 1970. People felt that their living standard was improving as a result of this industrial expansion. By 1970 about 90 percent of Japanese households owned a television, washing machine, and refrigerator, products considered luxury goods in the early 1960s (Katsuhara 1997). During the 1960s, Japan's sulfur dioxide emissions, chemical oxygen demand (COD), and industrial wastes also increased—by 3.5, 3.0, and 3.6 times, respectively (Eco Business Network 1995). Land development plans lacked environmental safeguards, and the national government intensively developed heavy industries in coastal areas.

Since residential areas were already located in the coastal areas, polluting factories were often established close to homes. Consequently, local residents suffered serious health problems in many industrial areas. Because of the worsening air pollution, residents began to protest in industrial cities. People became aware of health hazards as the mass media started to report on the pollution problem.

The national government had a plan to establish another petrochemical complex in Mishima and Numazu cities of the Shizuoka Prefecture. When the plan was disclosed, all the respective local governments welcomed it at first, but the local citizenry feared air pollution problems similar to problems being reported in other industrial cities. The national government claimed that the overall environmental impact of the petrochemical complex would be within acceptable levels. The mayor of Mishima City, however, decided to commission a study group composed of high school teachers and pollution experts to assess the environmental impact. Assessment results indicated that the environmental impact would be adverse. In 1964 more than 20,000 local citizens (one-third of the eligible voters) held a demonstration and demanded that the project be cancelled. As a result, the municipal governments changed their position and opposed the project. In the end the national government was forced to abandon the plan for a new petrochemical complex.

ENVIRONMENTAL QUALITY STANDARDS. In 1967 the national government established the Basic Law for Pollution Control. The object of this law was not to regulate any individual pollution source but to establish a basic framework for national policy on pollution control. This law, like the Soot and Smoke Control Law of 1962, referred to "undertaking living environmental management in harmony with sound industrial development." The authority for implementing the Basic Law for Pollution Control was not given to a single government ministry; rather, implementation responsibilities were dispersed among ten governmental agencies.

Although the basic law had limited efficacy in improving Japan's environmental quality in urban areas, it contained important measures that later contributed to the protection of the environment. In particular, it established ambient environmental quality standards (EQSs). In 1969 the following standards for sulfur dioxide in ambient air were set after vigorous discussions: (1) the number of hourly values less than 0.2 ppm exceeds 99 percent of the whole number of observed hourly values throughout the year; (2) the number of days when a daily average of hourly values is less than 0.05 ppm exceeds 70 percent of the observed days throughout the year; (3) the number of hourly values less than 0.1 ppm exceeds 88 percent of the whole number of observed hourly values throughout the year; and (4) the annual average of the hourly values does not exceed 0.05 ppm throughout the year.[2]

Upon the establishment of the environmental quality standards, the National Cabinet grouped Japanese areas into four different categories depending on social and environmental factors (such as population density and sulfur dioxide concentration in ambient air). It then set a target year for the attainment of the EQS in each category area. The EQS for sulfur dioxide should be attained within ten years in large industrial cities, within five years in medium-size industrial cities, and as soon as possible in other areas.

AIR POLLUTION CONTROL LAW OF 1968. In time the national government recognized that the Soot and Smoke Control Law of 1962 was failing to control emissions of sulfur oxides from factories and nitrogen oxides from automobiles. To replace the 1962 law, it established the Air Pollution Control Law of 1968. This new law was markedly different from the old one. In particular, area designations were abolished, making all areas subject to pollution controls; toxic substances (such as cadmium and chlorine) were designated as air pollutants; polluters could be punished; and prefecture governors were allowed to introduce ordinances with more stringent regulations than national ones, except for the emission standards for sulfur oxides. Also, the Air Pollution Control Law of 1968 abolished uniform emission standards for the sulfur oxides concentration of flue gas. Instead the law established standards based on the location and the stack height of the emission source.

POLLUTION CONTROL DIET SESSION. In the 1970s, public awareness of pollution increased even in relatively unpolluted areas. The mass media launched antipollution campaigns, and the derisive term "pollution archipelago" became well known throughout Japan. The media campaigns and increased pollution awareness changed people's attitude toward the environment. Citizens no longer regarded pollution as a purely local matter but as a problem for the entire nation to address. Asthma patients living near industrial complexes or along national roads filed lawsuits demanding compensation for pollution-related illness.

Leftist politicians appealed to the people, claiming that the national government—ruled by the conservative Liberal Democratic Party (LDP) since 1955—had polluted the country and that the environment would be improved only by electing leftist politicians and supporting leftist policies. As environmental awareness increased, urban citizens increasingly chose leftists to run their local governments. For example, in Yokohama, Tokyo, and Kawasaki, leftist politicians were elected to office, replacing conservative governors and mayors. These new leaders enforced stringent measures to control pollution.

Concerned that citizens' support for his party and its pro-industry policies was diminishing, Prime Minister Eisaku Sato convened the "Pollution Control Diet Session" in November 1970. This session passed fourteen environmental conservation bills. A symbolic result of the session was the deletion, from the Basic Law for Pollution Control, of the controversial provision on harmonization "of living environmental management with sound industrial development." The Environment Agency also was established to unify the administration of environmental policies in Japan. In a short time national policy on the environment changed direction.

The director general of the Environment Agency, Buichi Ohishi, warned that the iron mills would be shut down if their polluting practices continued unchecked. This threat astonished Isao Mizuno, the director of the Yahata Works of Nippon Steel, Japan's largest iron mill. Because the iron and steel industries had been the leading industries in Japan for such a long time, they were very influential politically and never imagined that a Cabinet member would challenge them (Terao 1998). Suddenly the industries realized that political sentiment had shifted against them because of the public's demand for a cleaner environment.

COURT CASES ON POLLUTION-RELATED DISEASES. According to the "traditional" interpretation of Japanese law, plaintiffs had to prove the cause-effect relationship between pollution and health damage. Lacking sufficient scientific data, plaintiffs had difficulty winning their cases. In 1970, however, the Supreme Court presented the lower courts with a new interpretation of the law. The respective responsibilities of the disputing parties changed. Once a certain relationship between polluting activities and health damage was established, the defendants would become liable for the damage.

Japanese businesses lost in four successive court cases in the early 1970s regarding compensation for pollution-related diseases: Itai-itai disease (caused by eating rice contaminated with cadmium), Niigata Minamata disease (caused by eating fish contaminated with organic mercury); asthma (caused by air pollution) in Yokkaichi City; and Minamata disease. In the asthma case the relationship between pollution and health damage was epidemiologically identified (Kuroda 1996, 67–74). If ambient air was significantly polluted by local factories and local citizens suffered from pollution despite factories' compliance with the national emission standards (the case in Yokkaichi), the factories were liable for health damages. Hence in the Yokkaichi pollution lawsuit in 1972, the plaintiffs won their case.

NEW CONSENSUS AMONG INDUSTRIES. Until the 1960s, industries in Japan were primarily concerned with labor issues and gave little thought to environmental issues. The industries were aware that their production activities were polluting the environment, but they thought it was unavoidable. However, in the early 1970s, the national government enacted several antipollution measures. Subsequently, businesses made intensive investments in pollution control in the mid-1970s (see Figure 2.3). The line graph in this figure shows the ratio of pollution control investments to total investments per year for big businesses (those with capital of over 100 billion yen). Steel and chemical industries rapidly increased their investment in pollution control during the first half of the

1970s. The bar graph in Figure 2.3 shows the production (nominal) of pollution control equipment in Japan in the period 1970 to 1985, as reported by the Japan Industrial Machinery Association.

Once Japan's enterprises reached a consensus on the necessity of controlling pollution, they took concerted action. Pollution control and energy savings even became the subject of competition within certain enterprises. These enterprises increased their profitability despite the huge expenses they incurred by adopting pollution control measures. Manufacturing industries actually strengthened their competitiveness in the world market through improved pollution control and energy efficiency.

Period of Oil Shocks

From the 1960s until the beginning of the 1970s, the Japanese economy grew dramatically by developing heavy industries dependent upon cheap petroleum. Japan depended on foreign sources for 90 percent of its primary energy needs. It was thus heavily burdened by the first oil shock that occurred in October 1973. The price of crude oil (Arabian light), which had remained stable at US$2 to US$3 per barrel during the 1960s, suddenly rose to about US$12 per barrel by 1974 (Yahata Works 1982). As Japanese consumers panicked, the prices of major commodities jumped by 14.6 percent in 1974. Cutbacks in governmental expenditures, policies adopted to fight inflation, pushed the Japanese economy into a depression, and economic growth turned negative in 1974.

In November 1973 the national government requested a 20 percent reduction in energy consumption of the business sector and energy savings by citizens. Enterprises were able to survive by reducing manufacturing costs through increased energy savings. For example, Nippon Steel succeeded in achieving a 10.4 percent reduction in energy consumption within four and a half years.[3]

Figure 2.3 *Pollution Control Investment and Equipment Production*

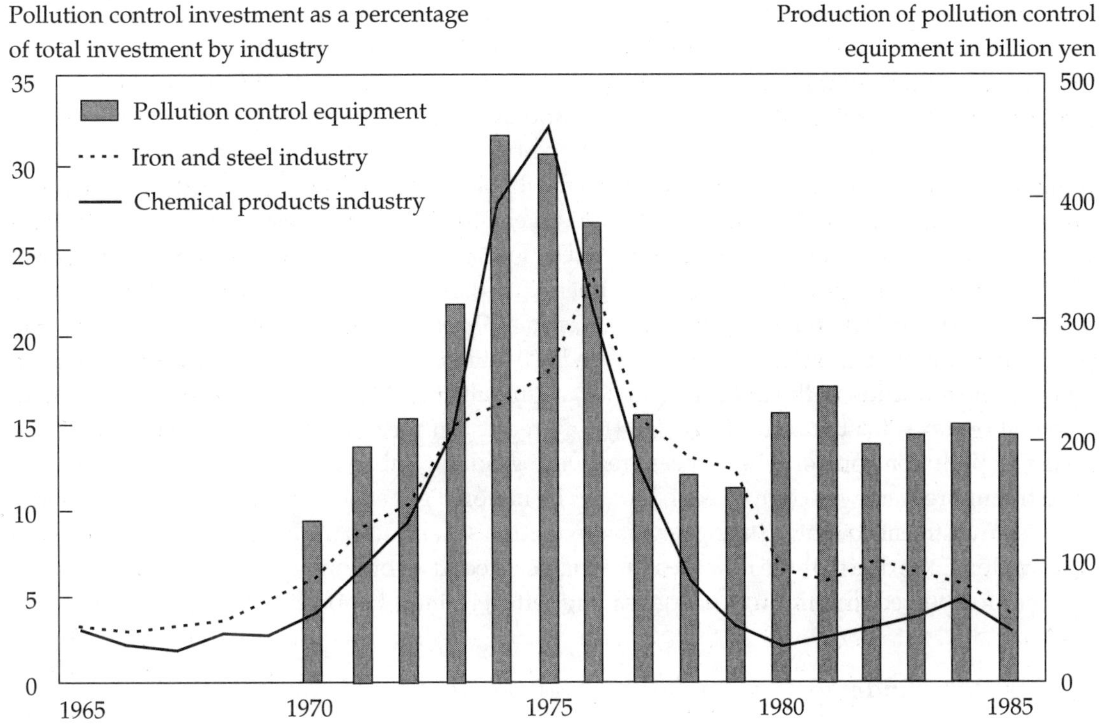

Pollution control investment as a percentage of total investment by industry

Production of pollution control equipment in billion yen

Source: MITI (various years) and Japan Industrial Machinery Association (various years).

Its petroleum consumption for the production of one ton of crude steel declined from 120.8 liters in 1973, to 89.0 liters in 1978, to 59.3 liters in 1979 (Yahata Works 1982). At the same time, energy-saving activities in Japanese industries significantly reduced the emission of air pollutants. The Environment Agency estimated that energy savings contributed to around 40 percent of the total reduction in sulfur oxides emissions in Japan in 1986 (Environment Agency 1990, 128).

MITI's Low-Sulfur Program. As early as the mid-1960s, MITI became concerned about industrial pollution. It felt that worsening pollution would intensify citizens' movements against industrial development and hinder implementation of its industrial policies. As long as fuel was very cheap for Japanese industries, energy conservation was not pursued as a way to reduce sulfur dioxide emissions. During the 1960s, flue gas desulfurization technology was not yet available, so importing low-sulfur crude oil was the only feasible option to reduce emissions at that time.

The first oil shock in 1973, however, changed the picture. The approach of lowering sulfur content to reduce emissions became difficult with constraints on oil supply. Subsequently, by providing economic incentives (tax exemptions and concessional loans from the Japan Development Bank), MITI promoted research and development of desulfurization technologies and installation of oil desulfurizers.

Economic Instruments to Control Emissions. Neither emission charges nor taxes were used in Japan to control emissions. An emission charge on sulfur oxides was introduced, but it was to compensate patients suffering from pollution related-diseases (under the Law for Pollution-Related Damage Compensation of 1973). Instead of using direct economic charges or taxes, the national government provided economic incentives to facilitate factories' adoption of antipollution and energy savings measures. These incentives included soft loans by public financial institutions and local governments, and tax exemptions.

The soft loan program is discussed in detail in Chapter 5, so we focus on the tax measures in this section. The Basic Law for Pollution Control, as well as the Air Pollution Control Law and the Water Pollution Control Law, stipulated that the national government should encourage pollution control investments through financial support and tax exemptions or reductions accorded to industries. Among various tax measures, reduction of the depreciation term seemed to be effective, particularly for the SMIs. Since it was difficult for the SMIs to have a long-term perspective, they preferred to complete the repayment of their investment loans as soon as possible while business was profitable. This tax measure was widely adopted by local governments (Osaka City is one example). SMIs supported it, although the measure did not reduce the overall amount of taxes they had to pay.

Decreases in tax revenues of the national government, due to tax reduction measures intended to promote pollution control investments, reached 100 billion yen in 1975. Of this amount, 60 billion yen was the reduction in the direct national tax, equivalent to 20 percent of the total reduction in corporation taxes for the year (Terao 1994). Tax reduction measures encouraged businesses to invest in pollution control. These measures were gradually abandoned after the antipollution investment program was completed in Japan. The national government later encouraged energy savings investments by introducing new tax reduction schemes. In the late 1980s, the decrease in corporation taxes due to these new measures had exceeded 70 billion yen per year, and air pollution was further reduced through energy savings efforts (Terao 1994)

Factors that Hindered Environmental Management

Proper management of the environment by Japanese industry was hindered until the 1970s by three main factors: the public's lack of awareness of the dangers of pollution, the government's lack of commitment to pollution control, and inadequate technology and scientific knowledge.

Lack of Public Awareness of Pollution

Until the mid-1960s, most people in Japan were not concerned about protecting the environment or aware of the hazards pollution could pose to their health. Without public pressure, both the local and national governments had little incentive to enact regulations for pollution control and environmental management. The majority of the population considered pollution, particularly air pollution, as an unavoidable outcome of industrialization. As noted earlier, black smoke was viewed with pride in their communities as a symbol of local development. Many Japanese had no idea what pollution was. When Bunbei Hara became the first president of the Japan Environment Corporation in 1965, he had to explain the meaning of *kogai* (pollution) to those who came to celebrate his promotion and why environmental cooperation was necessary (JEC 1976).

Fishermen and farmers whose livelihoods were directly affected by pollution began to initiate public protests. Yokkaichi fishermen, for example, demanded that polluting companies compensate them because the effluent from the factories was polluting their fishing areas. Other local citizens followed suit and started to complain about air pollution and offensive odors.

A consensus in the business community on the importance of pollution control was not reached until the 1970s. Before then, national politics had a pro-business rather than a pro-environment slant. As an example, Mr. Michio Hashimoto of the Ministry of Health was warned by his service superior not to go too far on air pollution control. Pressures from the business community and lack of public demand for cleaner air were the reasons for opposition to strict control measures. When Mr. Hashimoto became the national officer in charge of pollution control, he was sometimes criticized as *aka* (communist) by businesspeople.

Lack of Commitment by Government to Environmental Management

Until the 1960s, the primary objective of the national government was rapid economic development, and it sought to attain this by expanding heavy industries. The national government clearly valued economic development over environmental management. All laws established during the 1960s, including the Soot and Smoke Control Law of 1962 and the Basic Law for Pollution Control of 1967, contained articles ensuring "sound economic development." The goal of these laws was to "improve" polluted areas. The legislation failed to "prevent" pollution.

Environmental issues were seldom taken into account in the development of land use plans and during economic planning. In the 1970s, the national government changed its policy focus from pro-business to pro-environment only when citizens' movements became intense throughout the country. The media began to stress the negative impact on the environment of Japan's industrial policy, and conservative heads of local governments began to be replaced by leftist politicians one after another in major industrial areas.

Lack of Technology and Scientific Knowledge

Air quality was continuously monitored in some industrial areas, such as Kitakyushu, in the 1950s. In general, however, monitoring emissions was a difficult task for local governments to undertake, and the monitoring data were often insufficient to establish a solid scientific case for pollution control measures. In Yokohama, Kitakyushu, and Osaka, scientific data helped the municipal governments persuade local factories to cut down emissions, institutions for pollution control studies were established in each of these cities. The responsibility of each factory for local air pollution was made clear, and the factories subsequently adopted antipollution measures.

Controlling emissions of sulfur oxides was technically difficult; removing dust was relatively easily attained through several methods, such as switching from the use of coal to oil, increasing burning efficiencies, and/or installing precipitators or filters. Both oil and flue gas desulfurization technologies were not available until the late 1960s, when Japanese industry was heavily dependent on high-sulfur oil imported from the Middle East. Therefore, the national standard for sulfur oxide emissions was set at a very lax level of 2,200 ppm.

Factors that Enabled Environmental Management

What explains the shift in Japan's national policy away from economic development and toward environmental management? This section addresses this question. Five factors are noteworthy: Japan's democratic system, the influence of the mass media, decisionmaking by local governments, consensus building among stakeholders, and the attitude of business.

Democratic System

For proper control of pollution, a political system is needed in which the wishes of the majority are reflected in governmental decisionmaking. Victims of industrial pollution are usually vulnerable politically and economically. Polluting industries tend to reward the powerful capitalist and managerial classes, but the negative consequences of environmental degradation are passed on primarily to the weak. Managers of industry can live in neighborhoods with clean air and water and commute to their polluting factories, while poor laborers usually live near the factories where the environment is not clean and the rent is cheap. A government whose priority is to gain the support of the powerful through economic development policies is likely to be disinterested in environmental conservation policies benefiting a powerless majority.

As long as ordinary citizens in Japan accepted a polluted environment without protest, the government had little incentive to effect any changes. Few nongovernmental organizations were influential. Pollution control became an issue only after protests by citizens. Even when they felt dissatisfied with their polluted environment, Japanese citizens were often reluctant to speak out, fearing that their communities would regard them unfavorably as troublemakers. But when pollution worsened to the point that it clearly jeopardized living conditions and public health, the benefits of undertaking environmental collective action finally exceeded the costs. Then collective action became "the most crucial determining factor" in Japan's environmental management (Ui 1989). The complaints of the victims and the concerns of ordinary citizens were not taken into consideration in national government policies until the late 1960s. Some local governments had already initiated substantial pollution control measures by that time.

Mass Media

The independence of mass media from control by government is also indispensable to the establishment of proper pollution control. In Japan the media supported leftists' local governments by reporting their efforts to fight "polluting industries" at a time when the national government was still reluctant to engage in such action. Both at the local and national levels, freedom of the media prompted politicians to enforce substantive antipollution measures. Newspapers supported measures taken by the leftist mayor of Yokohama, Mr. Asukata, and local newspapers repeatedly criticized the "slow" environmental improvement in Kitakyushu. The conservative mayor of Kitakyushu, Mr. Tani, and his senior officials claimed that criticism by newspapers was what had most influenced them to institute controls.

At the national level, newspapers actively encouraged public support for Buichi Ohishi, the second director general of the Environment Agency. Conservative politicians in the ruling LDP were still pro-industry. Because of his environmental agenda, Mr. Ohishi, an LDP member himself, was sometimes isolated in the Cabinet. With the support of the mass media and sometimes with the backing of the opposition parties, however, he was able to direct the Environment Agency and move forward the implementation of environmental policies.

Newspapers swayed not only politicians but also bureaucrats in the national government. Despite efforts of the MITI to reduce sulfur oxide emissions, newspapers laid all of the administrative responsibility for air pollution problems on this ministry. A former MITI officer said that newspapers' criticisms of MITI had encouraged it to enforce antipollution measures.

Information raised public awareness of the need to control pollution. Both local and national governments disclosed information about pollution, particularly after the 1970s, even though these disclosures led to accusations by the media and local citizens that government actions were inadequate. It was thus difficult for the government, but crucial for proper environmental management, to disclose information.

Local Governments

Because the political heads of local governments in Japan are chosen by direct local elections, governors and mayors have to listen carefully to the will of the local majority when establishing regulatory policies. National government politicians are commonly controlled by bureaucratic bottom-up decision-making, but local leaders have ultimate control over personnel affairs and budgetary decisions. As a result, local leaders are able to directly determine local policy. They have an unmistakable impact on local administration and can take quick and definitive action.

The effectiveness of local government leaders in Japan in controlling pollution tended to be enhanced by the expertise of engineers. To address the problems caused by polluting sources scattered across the country, engineers were invaluable. Because the Japanese regard higher education in science and technology as important, most national universities in every prefecture have faculties of science and/or engineering. There have been many engineers in Japan. Since there is no significant wage gap between the public and private sectors, local governments have been able to recruit competent staff from these institutions. Furthermore, on-the-job training and lifelong employment ensure that these local officials are both well trained and well equipped to implement the policies of local leaders. They have the knowledge needed to monitor the local environment and to instruct factories about pollution control measures.

Consensus Building

Pollution control can be achieved only when it is integrated into all relevant policies.[4] Close collaboration among government agencies is essential. In Japan real consensus is required to establish any laws or national policies. Once something is decided in the government, it is enforced by all the relevant agencies, even those that may have opposed the policy during the negotiation stage.

This reliance on consensus in decisionmaking is time consuming, particularly with regard to unprecedented policy. In many cases an innovative policy is emasculated during the long negotiating and lobbying process. Pollution control policies were no exception. It was very hard for the officers of the Ministry of Health to overcome the compartmentalized national bureaucracy.[5] Every law concerning pollution control that was passed during the 1960s was drastically weakened during negotiations. As a result, an effective national policy on the environment could not be reached for many years.

However, once the government adopted specific pollution control policies in the early 1970s, all government agencies backed them up. Although MITI was reluctant to agree to proposed legislation to control pollution because of concerns that economic development would be hindered, it substantially changed its policy after 1970 and even made use of the new environmental policy to promote industrial development.

When the Environment Agency submits a newly drafted environmental policy to other government agencies, line ministries solicit the opinions of industrial organizations, which express their opinions on the feasibility of the policy during this formulation process. If a very stringent emission standard is needed, measures necessary to secure proper implementation by industry are considered. A step-by-step approach to achieving the desired standard may be adopted. NGOs and local residents in favor of stringent measures are often dismayed when the "good" draft has its teeth removed. However, this process of reaching consensus promotes implementation. A target set too high may discourage industries from even attempting to meet it.

Attitude of Business

Once consensus within industry on the need for pollution control was achieved in Japan, competition to reduce emissions followed. For example, managers of Nippon Steel's factories throughout Japan added interfactory pollution control competitions to their traditional productivity competitions. Managers devoted themselves to the development of new pollution control technology because winners would have a greater chance of promotion.

The attitudes of Japanese manufacturing industries contributed to improvements in the environment. In fiscal year 2000, there were 2,360 environmental law violations: 2,319 waste treatment violations (primarily dumping of wastes generated from construction), 7 violations of water quality laws, and 34 violations of other laws (Environment Agency 2001). Manufacturing enterprises have improved their environmental record under the guidance of their local governments. If a violation is discovered, the enterprise will be targeted as a "polluting industry" and looked upon with scorn by the community. Enterprises care about their social status and try hard to avoid being branded as a "polluter."

Traditionally, factory engineers have enjoyed high status in their companies; they have been eager to develop new and innovative technologies, including those to control pollution and conserve energy. Engineers' efforts are appreciated even in routine work, such as waste treatment, which does not increase productivity directly. A national certification of "pollution control manager" has contributed to the prestige of engineers. Every factory is required by law to have a pollution control manager.

Part II. Pollution Control Measures of Municipal Governments

Before the national government implemented serious measures to control pollution, municipal governments in major industrial cities pursued their own initiatives to reduce air pollution. Three industrial cities—Yokohama, Kitakyushu, and Osaka—have already been investigated as case studies by the Metropolitan Environment Improvement Program (MEIP 1994). This section, therefore, focuses on the social and administrative factors that enabled the improvement in pollution from sulfur oxides.[6]

In all three cities the municipal governments were pressured by a growing number of citizens' complaints against air pollution, but they had limited authority for pollution control because the Soot and Smoke Control Law delegated authority to the prefecture governments. Municipal governments were not authorized to monitor emissions or to inspect pollution sources located in their cities. It was only after passage of the Air Pollution Control Law of 1968, replacing the old law, that these cities were delegated the needed authority.

This section describes, in addition to the three industrial cities, the case of Yokkaichi City of Mie Prefecture. In this particular case, both the municipal and prefecture governments failed to control Japan's worst sulfur oxide pollution until 1972, when the local court required payment of compensation for health damages to Yokkaichi asthma patients. The introduction of total emission control by the prefecture government after the court decision reduced pollution levels substantially. It also facilitated the introduction of similar measures at the national level.

Yokohama City

Air quality in Yokohama City was poor after World War II. During the late 1940s, U.S. military men and their families in Yokohama began to suffer from asthma and did not completely recover even after they returned to the United States. This illness became known as "Yokohama Asthma." Like other industrial cities in Japan, Yokohama City became even more polluted during the era of reconstruction and thereafter. Iron dust from iron mills penetrated through shut windows in houses and classrooms. The shirt collars of businesspeople turned black whenever they spent time outside. In some areas, laundry was not hung outside for drying because the mist of sulfuric acid made small holes in the clothes.[7]

PLAN FOR A NEW COAL-FIRED POWER PLANT. In 1964 Ichio Asukata defeated the incumbent conservative and became the mayor of Yokohama City. Mr. Asukata was a member of the Socialist Party. It claimed that the conservative and pro-business policies of LDP at the national and local government levels were responsible for polluting the country and that only leftist policies would improve the environment. Mr. Asukata, therefore, had a mandate to improve the environment, particularly air quality.

When Mr. Asukata took office, a coal-fired power plant had been planned for the Isogo area of the city—an area reclaimed from the sea by the municipal government during the former mayor's administration. One piece of the reclaimed land (ca. 300,000 square meters) had already been sold to Tokyo Electric Co. Ltd, which had a plan to establish an oil-fired power plant. Later it was decided by the national government that the Electric Power Development Company (EPDC) should purchase one-third of this land from Tokyo Electric Co. and establish a new coal-fired plant.

In those days local citizenry in the area intensely protested against air pollution caused by an oil refinery. Concerned that the proposed coal-fired power plant would worsen pollution, the municipal government assessed the environmental impact of the power plant using a wind-tunnel experiment and found that it would be significant. Under the Soot and Smoke Control Law, emissions from power plants were regulated by the MITI, which was in charge of Japanese energy policy. Neither prefectural nor municipal governments were authorized to control emissions.

THE YOKOHAMA METHOD. A land contract concluded between the Yokohama Municipal Government and Tokyo Electric Co. stipulated that the approval of the municipal government was required before the company could sell the land to a third party. This provision prevented the purchasers of land reclaimed by a public body from selling it to other parties seeking profits. Without the municipal government's approval, Tokyo Electric would not be able to sell land to the EPDC. Establishing a new coal power plant was a national policy, however, and it was difficult for a municipal government to directly oppose it. Moreover, the municipal government needed a new local tax source, and the labor union for the coal mine was a strong supporter of the mayor's Socialist Party. Instead of opposing the new plant, the municipal government obtained an agreement with MITI to negotiate with EPDC about the plant. Then it succeeded in reaching pollution control agreements with the EPDC; in exchange the city let EPDC purchase the land.

In those days precipitation technologies were available, but flue gas technology was not. Using low-sulfur coal was the only available method to control sulfur oxide emissions. Fortunately, domestic low-sulfur coal containing only 0.3 percent sulfur was available at a mine in Hokkaido. With this coal the sulfur oxide concentrations in flue gas would be about 250 ppm, far below the national standard of 2,200 ppm. Even if coal containing 1 percent sulfur was used, the sulfur oxide concentration would only be 500 ppm. Under the pollution control agreement, the municipal government required the EPDC to use low-sulfur domestic coal. In addition, EPDC had to adopt the best available technologies, reduce power generation during periods of serious air pollution, and allow inspection by municipal officers.

This innovative approach encouraged the municipal government to control pollution despite its limited authority to implement pollution control measures. The mass media accused the national conservative policy of the LDP of polluting Japan, but they unanimously supported Mr. Asukata as "a mayor combating against polluting companies." He often attended meetings held by citizens protesting pollution, and local citizens strongly supported him, believing that the municipal government would be able to solve the pollution problems.

As for the companies, they needed to expand production as the Japanese economy rapidly grew during the 1960s. Yokohama was one of Japan's most attractive areas for business. It has an international port and is located very close to Tokyo, the largest Japanese market. On the one hand, local citizens, often supported by local medical doctors, were speaking out against pollution. On the other hand, the companies needed some affirmation of their activities from the municipal government in order to win acceptance by the citizenry. The municipal government concluded pollution control agreements one after another whenever companies expanded their facilities and/or established new ones, thus successfully reducing sulfur oxide emissions (see Figure 2.4). Reaching pollution control agreements remained a popular approach for local governments even after they were delegated pollution control authority.[8] This approach became known as the Yokohama Method.

IMPLICATIONS OF THE YOKOHAMA METHOD. Mr. Asukata and the municipal government considered scientific knowledge and monitoring data indispensable in their efforts to convince factories to adopt adequate measures and enforce environmental policies. The municipal government developed and operated Japan's first air quality monitoring telemeter system using public telecommunication lines as early as 1966. It also established the municipal research institute for pollution control with thirty-five staff members. (Currently, the number of personnel exceeds seventy.)

Figure 2.4 *Sulfur Oxide Concentrations in Ambient Air*

Daily sulfur oxide concentrations in milligrams per 100 square centimeters

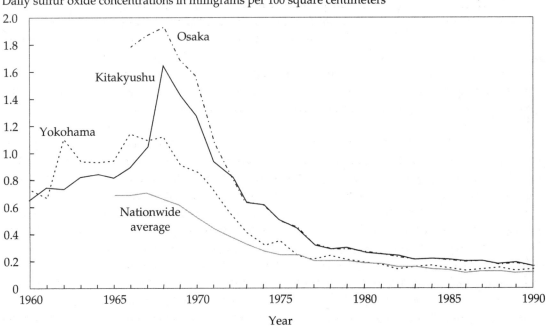

Source: MEIP (1994), Fujikura (1998), and Osaka (1998).

The legal basis of the pollution control agreements was seldom discussed. Some lawyers and companies doubted their effectiveness because the agreements were not based on enforceable laws. Mr. Asukata, a lawyer, insisted that the pollution control agreements were private contracts and that punishments could be specified for violators of the agreements. The companies observed the agreements because the agreements implied that they had obtained the city's approval for their activities and because the agreements ended citizens' protests.

Sulfur dioxide concentration in ambient air started to decrease in 1966. Actual emissions of sulfur oxides from large factories in an industrial area declined 60 tons per day in 1970, while that forecasted in 1966 was 300 tons a day.

This method was effective only for newly established facilities of large industries. The municipal government was not able to conclude agreements with existing facilities or with large numbers of small and medium-size industries. In dealing with them, the municipal government established a series of guidelines on each pollutant, such as sulfur oxides, nitrogen oxides, and noise, and shifted its focus from reaching pollution control agreements to implementing guidelines. The guidelines were not based on local ordinances, and they were established without any consultation with the local assembly. Recently, these guidelines were replaced by ordinances in order to reduce the number of guidelines and to make regulations simpler.

Kitakyushu City

Kitakyushu's major industries were iron and steel, chemical products, and stone and clay products. After air pollution in Ube City improved, the residential district of Shiroyama, surrounded by industrial areas, in Kitakyushu held the record in Japan for the worst dust fall from the late 1950s to the mid-1960s. A monthly record of 123.8 tons of dust fall per square kilometer was recorded in September 1966. Roofs caved in under the weight of the dust. Oily dust stuck to electric wires and formed "dust icicles." Every elementary school classroom was equipped with two air-cleaning machines. Sprinklers were installed in the playgrounds to prevent the dust from blowing into the classrooms. Pupils had to gargle every day using special "gargling equipment." Although the Kitakyushu schools took every possible measure for adequate health management, many pupils continued to suffer from pollution-related illnesses. The proportion of absentees in Tobata Ward schools from 1963 to 1965 always exceeded 10 percent and sometimes even exceeded 50 percent (Hayashi 1971, 111–18).

As industrial fuel in Kitakyushu City was switched from coal to petroleum and as consumption of petroleum increased, the coal dust problem was naturally solved (see Figure 2.2), but sulfur oxide concentrations in ambient air gradually increased (see Figure 2.4).

SILENT CITIZENS. Despite severe pollution, the local people did not protest. One of the reasons for the silence of Kitakyushu's citizens was their ignorance of the health effects of pollution. Most of the local citizens were factory laborers and their families, and they regarded smoke from the factories as a symbol of prosperity. People were particularly proud of the smoke from the Yahata Works, Japan's largest iron mill. Moreover, factory laborers did not regard Kitakyushu as a place to live but a place to work. Most of them had come from rural areas. They tended to return to their hometown villages and farms after retirement. Thus, their living environment was less important to them than the economic benefits they derived from working in the factories.

The Yahata Works dominated local politics and economics. Before the Second World War, the Yahata Works was a national iron mill, and it did not have to pay taxes to the city. It voluntarily "subsidized" local development projects such as water works, schools, and fire stations (Yahata Works 1980, 608–17; Hayashi 1971, 51–60). After the war the Yahata Works was privatized and became one of the Nippon Steel Corporation's iron works. However, the Yahata Works' influence remained unchanged from the prewar period. Two retired Yahata Works staff members served as mayors of Yahata City before the city became part of the newly formed Kitakyushu City in 1963. The relationship between the municipal government and the Yahata Works was closer than the relationship in other Japanese cities between businesses and the government. The majority of the residents were employees of these industries, or they were related to employees. Understandably, local citizens hesitated to do anything that might jeopardize their employers.

ROLE OF WOMEN IN RAISING AWARENESS OF POLLUTION. As time passed, an increasing number of laborers brought up their children and retired in Kitakyushu. As Kitakyushu became a place to call "home," a place to reside and not just to work, more people became concerned about its pollution. Women were the first to take action to address the problem. In the mid-1960s, they organized groups to study local pollution problems. The polluting enterprises quickly learned about the women's activities and used whatever means they could to stop them. Many of the husbands of the group members worked at the polluting factories, and the companies threatened them with transfers from their jobs.

The women did not challenge the enterprises directly. Instead they petitioned the municipal government to implement effective antipollution measures, and they backed up their petitions with the results from their pollution studies. They also reported these findings to the public. The women produced an eight-millimeter film about local industrial pollution to show to the public. Newspapers and television stations reported their activities. This stimulated a general awareness of the impact of local air pollution on human health and the environment. According to a survey conducted by the municipal government in 1971, 49.6 percent of the citizens became aware of "smog pollution."

MUNICIPAL SUPPORT FOR POLLUTION CONTROL MEASURES. Gohei Tani, the mayor of Kitakyushu, was a conservative politician supported by the conservative Liberal Democratic Party and by local industry. When he was first elected in 1967, he thought that pollution was strictly a matter for the prefectural government. However, as the general public became increasingly aware of pollution problems, citizens' complaints to the municipal government about air pollution increased: the number of complaints increased from an annual average of sixty-one during the 1960s to a record of 179 in 1971. Both the local media and municipal assembly members criticized Mr. Tani for "the delay in pollution control" and "loose antipollution regulations."

During the late 1960s, the local media and opposition party members of the municipal assembly compared Kitakyushu City unfavorably to other industrial cities governed by leftist politicians. A comparison of sulfur oxide concentrations in ambient air showed that improvement of air quality in Kitakyushu City was two years behind that of the socialist-governed Yokohama City (see Figure 2.4).

Pollution problems became the most important issue in the 1971 mayoralty election. Mr. Tani's rival, who was supported by the Communist Party, criticized his pro-business policies and appealed for more stringent pollution control. Mr. Tani was forced to counter this attack by proposing a progressive policy on pollution control. It was only through an intensive political campaign by the business community in support of Mr. Tani that he obtained 61 percent of the vote and was reelected. However, the number of votes for his rival was more than three times the number of local Communist Party supporters, an indication of strong support for his candidacy.

Both the severity of the pollution problems and the loss of popular support for conservative politicians forced Mr. Tani to take drastic antipollution measures. Having upgraded the eight-member Pollution Control Division in 1970 to a twenty-two-member Pollution Control Department in 1971, he upgraded the department to a forty-seven-member Pollution Control Bureau. While the mayor and senior municipal officials tried to counter criticisms from the media, these officials devoted themselves to enforcing measures that they believed would be the most effective in controlling pollution.

Local industry, like the mayor, gradually recognized that there was no alternative but to support the municipal government's increasingly progressive stance on pollution control. If pollution worsened, a leftist would replace the conservative mayor of Kitakyushu and might impose even more strict controls.

SCIENTIFIC DATA AS BASIS FOR STANDARDS. In 1970 the Fukuoka Prefectural Government and the Kitakyushu Municipal Government, in collaboration with the major industries of Kitakyushu, established the Joint Committee on Air Pollution Prevention in Kitakyushu. This joint committee included representatives of the thirty factories emitting 97 percent of the city's sulfur oxides. In order to meet the environmental quality standard for sulfur dioxide by fiscal 1973, the municipal government in 1972 concluded a First Agreement on pollution control with fifty-four factories. This agreement was based on agreements reached by the joint committee. Factories utilized higher smoke stacks, and the EQS was attained by 1973.

However, in 1973 the environmental quality standard was made three times more stringent than it had been, and ambient air quality in Kitakyushu was required to meet the new EQS within five years. The members of the joint committee concluded a new pollution control agreement (the Second Agreement) to reduce total emissions in Kitakyushu by one-third in order to meet the new EQS by 1977.

An important issue was the distribution among factories of the financial and operational burdens of the antipollution measures. What would be fair? A factory's burden should depend on its responsibility for the air pollution problems. However, factories did not know the degree to which their operations were responsible for pollution. In order to solve this problem, the municipal government utilized the results of a study carried out by the Ministry of International Trade and Industry.

In 1969 MITI started a Comprehensive Study on Industrial Pollution (CSIP) in the Kitakyushu area in order to forecast the environmental impact of a new industrial complex planned for Kitakyushu. This was Japan's first comprehensive environmental impact study. Data accumulated by the municipal government through continuous monitoring since the 1950s were utilized for this study. A fluorescent substance was sprayed from a helicopter in order to determine meteorological elements. Based on these data, a wind tunnel experiment was conducted, and each factory's share of responsibility for existing air pollution was determined.

Guided by the CSIP, the municipal government recommended that each factory adopt specific measures, such as installing higher smoke stacks (under the First Agreement) or switching permanently from high-sulfur to low-sulfur heavy oil (under the Second Agreement). A detailed plan for sulfur dioxide reduction based on the city's recommendations and prepared by each factory was described in the "Annex" of each agreement. If the factories wanted to change their plans, they had to consult with the municipal government beforehand. By utilizing the Annex, the municipal government was able to provide each factory with ongoing individualized and comprehensive administrative guidance.

Solid scientific findings were used to require factories to take specific antipollution measures. The only way for an industry to resist was to challenge the scientific data. One company carried out the same wind tunnel experiment at its own expense only to confirm that the city's data were correct. Because the data could not be disproved, local industry had no choice but to comply with the city's directives.

All local industries tacitly agreed that Nippon Steel, the largest company operating in Kitakyushu and their traditional leader, would represent them. As a result, the municipal government only needed to negotiate directly with the Yahata Works of Nippon Steel. Once the municipal government and Yahata Works reached an agreement on any antipollution measure, the other companies would comply with the agreement. The social conscience of the Yahata Works facilitated this process. The employees had always been socially elite and taken pride in their company's role in the local society. Once Yahata Works accepted the city's stringent antipollution measures as being necessary for the general welfare of the city, it persuaded the other enterprises to comply (Shikata 1991).

A mutual reliance and cooperative relationship continued to exist between industries and the municipal government. The Annexes of the pollution control agreements included trade secrets about raw materials, kinds of fuels, the sulfur content of these fuels, fuel consumption, maximum emissions, and other matters. Industries felt that they could trust the conservative municipal government to treat these Annexes as classified information. They feared these secrets might be disclosed to the public if their conservative mayor was replaced by a leftist. (All of the contents of pollution control agreements concluded in Yokohama City, governed by leftists, had been opened to the public.) Because of this concern about disclosure, mutual dependence and cooperation between industries and the municipal government in Kitakyushu increased.

ANTIPOLLUTION MEASURES. As industries were required to adopt pollution control measures throughout Japan, the demand for low-sulfur heavy oil increased, and the supply became insufficient. The price of low-sulfur heavy oil relative to high-sulfur heavy oil increased dramatically (see Figure 2.5). In 1969 one kiloliter of high-sulfur heavy oil cost 5,900 yen; one kiloliter of Indonesian heavy-oil containing only 0.3 percent sulfur cost 6,100 yen. The price difference amounted to only 3 percent. By 1973, however, this difference jumped to 61 percent (Yahata Works 1982).

Figure 2.5 *Prices of Low-Sulfur and High-Sulfur Heavy Oil*

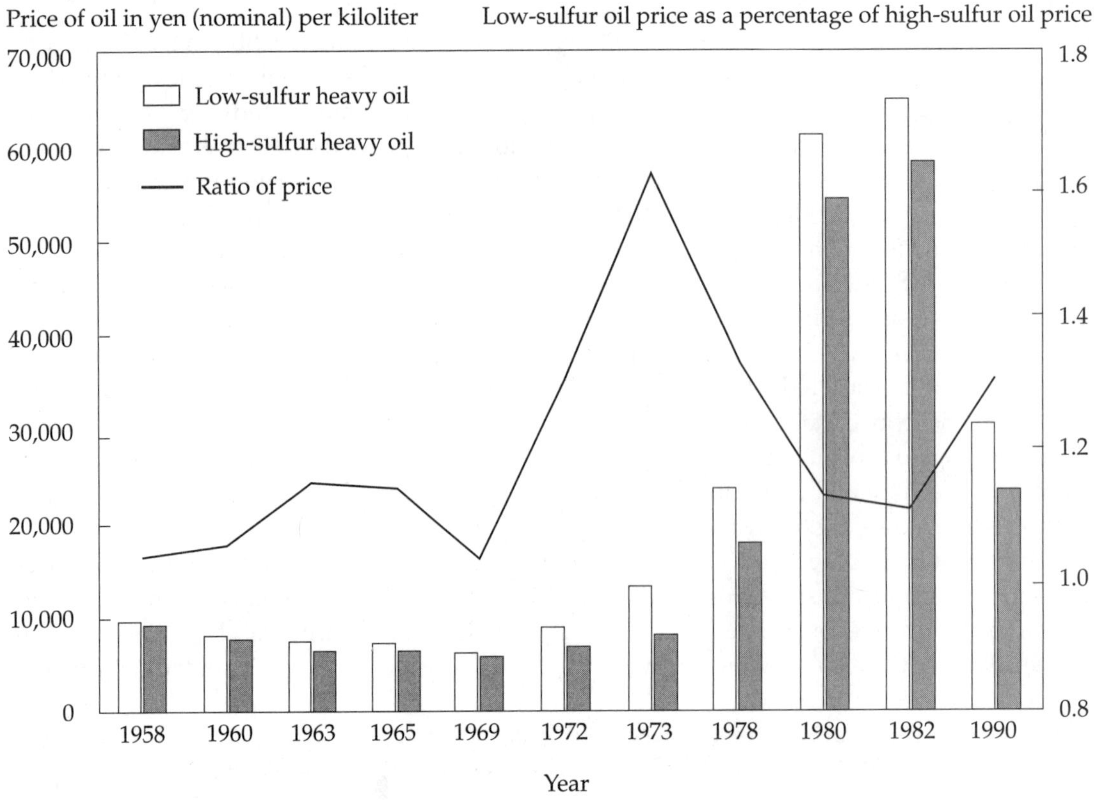

Price of oil in yen (nominal) per kiloliter   Low-sulfur oil price as a percentage of high-sulfur oil price

Source: Yahata Works (1982).

The difficulties of procuring low-sulfur fuel and its high cost inconvenienced Japanese industries. When the municipal government required a particular factory to reduce its sulfur dioxide emissions to one-sixth between 1970 and 1975, the factory estimated that the additional expense of switching to low-sulfur oil would eliminate half of its profits. Despite strong opposition within the company, it nonetheless accepted the cost increase and changed fuels.

Desulfurization technology was nearly available by 1974, but the municipal government remained disinterested in flue gas desulfurizers. When a factory prepared a plan to install desulfurization equipment, the municipal government requested the installation of backup emergency equipment. It also asked for a commitment to stop the whole operation whenever the desulfurization equipment stopped functioning. Steel works that used coal or petroleum as a raw material were already equipped with desulfurization technologies, but for the Kitakyushu industries the switch to low-sulfur fuel was the only way to conform to the city's antipollution guidelines.

The switch to low-sulfur fuels and energy-savings efforts after the 1973 and 1978 oil shocks enabled Kitakyushu to reduce its sulfur dioxide emissions substantially. For example, the sulfur oxides emissions of the Yahata Works in 1990 were about 2.2 percent of the 1970 emissions. The switch to low-sulfur fuels and raw materials accounted for 42 percent, the largest share, of the emission reductions (see Figure 2.6). Energy savings and recycling accounted for 33 percent, and flue gas desulfurization, 25 percent (IES 1996). The sulfur dioxide concentrations of ambient air also decreased to satisfactory levels. Test results show that in all the monitoring stations, national environmental quality standards have been met since 1976.

Osaka City

In the seventeenth century Osaka City enjoyed special status among municipalities and was granted various autonomous authorities by the Japanese feudal government. For centuries the local communi-

Figure 2.6 *Sulfur Dioxide Emission Reductions at the Yahata Works*

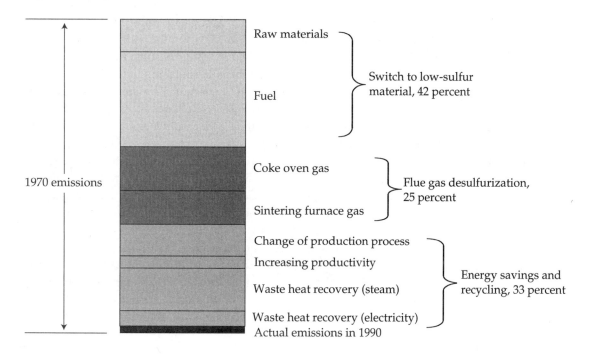

Source: IES (1996).

ties have played an important role in the "management" of the Osaka municipality. Since the postwar period, Local Development Associations (LDAs) have cooperated with the municipal ward office to enforce Osaka City's local policy. These associations have a pyramidal structure: the LDA is composed of local community unions, which are composed of local communities, which are composed of local citizens' "groups," and every family belonged to one local group. Merchants or factory owners were influential in local politics and were often appointed as directors of these local organizations.

Because of this cooperation between the municipal government and the local communities, citizens viewed the municipal government as their own organization and were seldom in conflict with it. Local businesses and citizens donated funds for a variety of projects in Osaka City.[9] In turn, the municipal government provided support to local industries, particularly small and medium-size industries, in various ways. For example, the municipal government financially supported local SMIs through soft loans. The Osaka Municipal Institute of Technologies granted its patents to SMIs without charge. This harmonious relationship between local businesses and the municipal government, a relationship not usually found in other municipalities, promoted effective measures for industrial pollution control in Osaka City.

AIR POLLUTION CONTROL MEASURES. In the mid-1950s, as during the prewar period, soot and smoke, which became known as "smog," again started to annoy residents of Osaka. One-fourth of the complaints about pollution in Osaka concerned smog. Most of the air pollution problems then were caused by coal dust. In the winter time thick smog, emitted from building heating systems, covered the downtown areas. The smog sometimes became so thick that it blocked sunlight, and drivers had to turn on their headlights even in the daytime. Local businesses understood the importance of adopting pollution control measures in order to protect human health and to improve the city's air quality.

The municipal government encouraged local businesses to organize the Soot and Smoke Prevention Cooperation Association, and the first association was established in 1958 in the Higashi Ward. Later associations were established in every ward, and the Osaka Alliance of these associations was established in 1960. The associations, like the Osaka Soot and Smoke Prevention Study Commission in the prewar period, investigated antipollution technologies and raised the business community's awareness of environmental concerns. Through this informal, rather than legal, mechanism, the municipal government was able to guide local factories.

When the Soot and Smoke Control Law was established in 1962, the authority to control air pollution was delegated to the prefectural governors, and the municipal mayor was not given any authority to control pollution. Although the guidance given to factories by the municipal government lacked a legal basis, the mayor, Mr. Chuma, continued to give it. Most factories allowed inspections by the local officers without questioning the legal basis of their activities. Only a few refused to be inspected. Even the power plants and gas plants permitted the inspections and followed the guidance, even though power and gas plants were not subject to the Soot and Smoke Control Law. (Other laws gave the MITI control over their emissions.) The municipal government was the largest stockholder of the Kansai Electric Corporation. The Osaka Gas Corporation, originally the Municipal Gas Department, was later privatized. The municipal government was able to control air pollution from the power plant and the gas plant without any difficulties.

When the Soot and Smoke Control Law was fully enacted in 1963, the Osaka Prefecture Government delegated to the municipal government the authority to enforce it. The law allowed prefectural governors to delegate their authority to municipalities, but prefectural governments usually resisted this. In Osaka the prefecture government recognized the effectiveness of implementing antipollution measures under the municipal government and therefore decided to delegate its authority.

ADMINISTRATIVE GUIDANCE. The municipal government prepared an Administrative Guidance Plan based on solid scientific data and made the plan open to the public. Then the municipal government held meetings to explain its policy to the local business community and to convey information about air pollution and health damages, antipollution technologies, soft loans, factory relocation as an antipollution measure, tax exemptions, the supply of low-sulfur heavy oil, and other issues.

The factories, including the SMIs, that attended the meetings understood the necessity of adopting measures to control air pollution, and they were able to prepare their own antipollution plan. After convening the meetings, the municipal government presented an emission reduction target for individual facilities, and it asked the facilities to submit their own Plan for Air Pollution Prevention. Through this individual guidance, the municipal government succeeded in lowering air pollution in Osaka.

THE BLUE SKY PROGRAMS. In the Osaka and Amagasaki areas, like in Kitakyushu, the MITI conducted a Comprehensive Study on Industrial Pollution (CSIP). The ministry forecast air pollution in Osaka Prefecture in 1972 based on emissions data from ninety-five large factories in the prefecture and on the results of a wind tunnel experiment. The maximum concentration of sulfur oxides on the ground could be reduced by approximately 30 to 40 percent if heavy oil in these factories was switched to heavy oil with a sulfur content of less than 1.7 percent. Then, in June 1969, the prefecture government established the first Blue Sky Program, and the municipal government gave guidance to large factories in order to attain the target.

Building heating systems in downtown Osaka City significantly contributed to local air pollution. Even if all large factories attained their emission reduction targets and the other facilities complied with the newly established emission standards of the Air Pollution Control Law, the environmental quality standard for sulfur oxides appeared unattainable. Thus, the municipal government established the Second Blue Sky Program in October 1969. The program's purpose was to reduce emissions from nonproduction facilities. The municipal government guided owners of buildings located in the downtown areas to switch their fuel to heavy oil containing less than 1.0 percent sulfur. Except for a few cases, most of the building owners were cooperative and switched their fuel once they understood the necessity of the measures.

EMERGENCY MEASURES IN THE NISHIYODOGAWA WARD. In the Nishiyodogawa Ward of Osaka City, small factories were built close to residential houses. Not surprisingly, there were plenty of complaints about air pollution. Monitoring of ambient air quality began in 1964, and the monthly average for emissions of sulfur oxides sometimes exceeded 0.2 ppm. In 1970, 653 citizens were officially designated as patients suffering from pollution-related diseases.

In 1966 a monitoring station was established at every block of 400×400 meters, and the 230 factories that had installed a smoke stack were inspected. Based on the data obtained from this study and on simulation analysis, the municipal government estimated the contribution of each factory to local air pollution. Using the results of the study, it guided the factories on how they should address the pollution problem. In order to implement emergency measures, the municipal government organized the Special Guard for Nishiyodogawa Ward Pollution Control. Thirteen local officers formed this guard.

The target of the emergency measures was to attain within two years the EQS for sulfur dioxide of 0.05 ppm. (The national government target for a similar EQS was attainment within ten years.) The pollution control measures commenced in 1970. The ambient concentration at 0.083 ppm in 1969 decreased to 0.042 ppm by 1972. The municipal government thus succeeded in reaching its target within two years.

THE KEYS TO SUCCESS IN OSAKA CITY. The Yokohama Method described earlier in this chapter was widely viewed as an effective tool for pollution control. Leftist parties in the municipal assembly, the mass media, and academicians repeatedly demanded that the Osaka Municipal Government adopt the Yokohama Method. However, the municipal government refused and continued instead to give administrative guidance to factories. It should be noted that the Yokohama Method was not intended to control pollution from existing factories that had no plan to expand or renovate their production facilities.

Reliance on Administrative Guidance. The municipal government argued against pollution control agreements as too restrictive. If the municipal government reached an agreement with factories, it would not be able to request any additional measures to control pollution, even when better technologies than those already subscribed to in the agreements were developed. The municipal government feared that pollution control agreements would become a sort of "indulgence," allowing factories to operate without adopting the "best" measures arrived at in a dynamic situation of antipollution technology development.[10] For these reasons the municipal government opted to institute administrative guidance instead of pollution control agreements.

Cooperation between the Government, Business, and Citizens. The good relations between the municipal government, local businesses, and citizens enabled substantial pollution control in Osaka City. Local businesses participated in the management of the municipality and generously gave donations for the development of the city. Small industries were technically and financially supported by the municipality and consequently felt indebted to it. They readily invested in antipollution measures once they understood the pollution problem and the degree to which they were responsible for it.

Company owners and factory managers often served as directors of local organizations such as the Local Development Associations mentioned earlier. These groups served as the forum for citizens' complaints about pollution. Complaints were submitted to the municipal government through the local organizations. Often the directors of groups voicing complaints were also the polluters of the local environment. Therefore, they adopted antipollution measures to hold their prestige in the community.

Once the municipal government officially received an antipollution plan from a factory, it asked citizens to endure the pollution until the plan was implemented. Citizens trusted the municipal government and usually waited patiently for improvements. Demonstrations and sit-ins did occur, but the municipal government believed the participants were organized by leftist political groups as part of their antigovernment campaign. In its view, few of the protesters were actually residents who were affected adversely by pollution. Therefore, the municipal government concentrated on dealing with complaints submitted through the local communities.

Initiatives of the Mayor. Both Kaoru Chuma, the mayor during the 1960s, and his successor, Yasushi Oshima, the mayor during the 1970s, were conservative, and they were widely supported by the local citizens. Osaka's leftist governor and mayors in other industrial cities, such as Yokohama and Tokyo, enjoyed less grass-roots support.

The mayor of Osaka City understood that the municipal government had to address the air pollution problem. Polluting factories were given incentives to adopt antipollution measures. Since the 1960s, pollution control measures had been the most important focus of the municipal government, and the mayor actively expanded environmental divisions to control air pollution. In 1975 the number of staff involved in pollution control reached 192. These initiatives of the mayor were welcomed by the local citizens.

Financial Support. A unique facility of Osaka for purchasing factories' land encouraged pollution control among small and medium-size industries. A number of factories in Osaka City owned by SMIs were on land too small to install pollution control equipment that was effective; hence, to address the pollution problem, they had to relocate or shut down. According to a study by the municipal government in 1968, 182 factories opted for relocation of the 290 factories that had caused (or may have caused) pollution-related complaints from local citizens. Under Osaka's facility for purchasing land, the municipal government bought the lots vacated after factories of SMIs relocated to other areas. By 1991 the municipal government had bought a total area of 192,780 square meters from seventy-two factories. Some of this land acquired by the municipal government became municipal parks or was used for community centers.

Through Osaka's facility for purchasing land, SMIs were able to obtain funds to acquire new land to relocate and sometimes to build new production facilities. The municipal government bought land in the city at the market price, much higher than the price of the new land where it relocated. Sometimes the municipal government also assessed the environmental impact of industrial operations at the new site instead of the assessment being done by the local government responsible for the site; this was because local government officials trusted the capability of the municipal government in pollution control matters.

Yokkaichi City

During the prewar period, light industries, such as textile and light machinery production, were the major industries in the Tokai region, which includes Yokkaichi City of the Mie Prefecture.[11] In 1939 the Japanese navy established its fuel depot at Yokkaichi Harbor, and an oil refinery station began operating in 1941. These facilities were completely destroyed during the war. In 1955 the Cabinet decided to hand over this place to Mitsubishi Corporation and Shell Group to establish a large-scale petrochemical complex. In 1959 the whole complex, which included an oil refinery, chemical product industries, and an oil-fired thermal power plant, started operations.[12] It was the largest petrochemical complex in Asia.

Until the early 1960s, industries in the Tokyo-Yokohama industrial area consumed domestic coal mined in the Tohoku and Hokkaido regions (northeastern Japan), and industries in Osaka and Kitakyushu were dependent on coal from the Kyushu region. The Tokai region was located far from all of the coal mines, and thus the price of coal in the region was expensive. As a result, the Yokkaichi area was already dependent on imported oil in the early 1960s. In 1962 oil as a percentage of all industrial fuel was 39.8 percent for Japan as a whole but 88 percent for Yokkaichi.

SULFUR OXIDE POLLUTION. According to an estimation of sulfur dioxide emissions in 1965, Yokkaichi City emitted annually 140 thousand tons (420 tons per day), exceeding Osaka's annual emissions of 110 thousand tons. All major sources of emissions in Yokkaichi were concentrated in a small area (about 30 square kilometers). Emissions were estimated to be ten times more intense than those in Osaka City.

Residential areas near the petrochemical complex had extremely serious pollution. In the early 1960s, an automatic measuring instrument installed in the Isozu area, the most polluted area, often recorded 1 ppm of sulfur dioxide in the ambient air; the worst record for the area was 2.5 ppm. In addition to sulfur oxides, the Yokkaichi area was polluted by sulfuric acid, and the acidity of rain water gradually increased from pH6 in 1961 to pH4 in 1967. Around the complex, soil became acidic with a pH less than 4.

YOKKAICHI ASTHMA. The first sign of air pollution recognized by the local residents was an offensive odor. As soon as factories in the complex began operating, complaints about an offensive odor were submitted to the municipal government. In the mid-1960s, the number of these complaints annually was more than 400 and accounted for more than 70 percent of total complaints concerning pollution. Chemicals emitted from oil refinery facilities, such as hydrogen sulfide and mercaptane, and various substances emitted from chemical factories were suspected to be the cause of the odor. The prefecture and municipal governments organized "patrol" groups to monitor the situation and suggested that factories should take remedial action. However, no effective measures were implemented by the factories.

As early as 1960, medical doctors reported an increase in cases of asthma in the Isozu area. The municipal government conducted a medical survey of more than 30,000 citizens. The survey found that cases of respiratory diseases and throat ailments were significantly more numerous in polluted areas than in unpolluted areas. Sukenori Hirata, the mayor of Yokkaichi City, allocated a special budget of 10 million yen in 1960 to treat asthma patients. This was Japan's first official measure to help designated patients of pollution-related illnesses. Mr. Hirata was a conservative politician, a member of the LDP. He believed that the city was able to develop its economy because of the petrochemical complex, and that the city, therefore, was obligated to share part of the benefits it derived from the complex with the victims.[13]

The mayor and the governor invited the petrochemical factories to Yokkaichi to develop the local economy. The factories became the mainstay of the local economy and were politically influential. They felt that it was unnecessary to adopt antipollution measures (because Yokkaichi was not designated as a pollution control area according to the Soot and Smoke Control Law)[14] and that factories were not subject to any national emission standards. Citizens in Yokkaichi appreciated the municipal government's effort to provide financial support to asthma patients. Local citizens were politically conservative. Few protests took place despite the worsening air and sickening population.

Kurokawa's Committee. In 1963 the Ministry of International Trade and Industry and the Ministry of Health organized an official committee (later called the Kurokawa Committee after the family name of the chairperson) to investigate the air pollution situation in Yokkaichi City, identify possible countermeasures, and examine whether the Yokkaichi area could be appropriately designated as a pollution control area. Because Yokkaichi had factories producing various chemicals and the sources of pollution were diverse, an interdisciplinary approach, relying on the production expertise of MITI and the health-related expertise of MHW, was needed.[15]

The business community strongly opposed committee recommendations to switch to low-sulfur fuel. The committee was not able to introduce emission standards for major facilities in the complex that were more stringent than the standards under the law (2,200 ppm). Despite strong opposition, a slightly more stringent standard was applied to the power plant, but this standard of 1,800 ppm was not strict enough to reduce pollution.

The factories did adopt the committee's recommendation to install higher smoke stacks to disperse emissions. Later this concept was included in the Air Pollution Control Law of 1967, and the K-value regulation was adopted as a standard. Constructing a higher stack was cheaper than installing flue gas desulfurizers. By 1967 almost all factories in the complex had smoke stacks 100 to 200 meters high. It was an effective measure to reduce local air pollution as long as the number of stacks was small. The measure reduced pollution in the Isozu area but spread it elsewhere. The polluted area increased from 20 percent of Yokkaichi City in 1965 to more than 50 percent in 1971.

Yokkaichi Litigation. Without effective measures to cut down emissions, the number of asthma patients increased. In 1964 an asthma patient died whose symptoms resembled the symptoms from "smog death" reported in London during the 1950s. Some despairing asthma patients committed suicide. In 1967 nine patients sued six factories in the complex, demanding compensation for their ruined health. During the trial, the factories insisted that they had been complying with national regulations and had installed the most advanced antipollution technologies.

The Tsu local court in 1972 decided in favor of the plaintiffs. It ruled that there was an epidemiological cause-and-effect relationship between air pollution and the respiratory diseases suffered by the plaintiffs. The activities of all of the factories in the complex were declared to be an illegal act. Even a factory that did not emit a significant amount of sulfur oxide was regarded as a part of the illegal activity of the whole complex as long as it utilized chemical products and electricity generated there. The court ruled that the factories were negligent in their responsibility to pay attention to the impact of their activities at the time, and it ordered the factories to pay 88.2 million yen as compensation for the damages inflicted on the plaintiffs (ICETT 1992). Although the factories were unsatisfied with the ruling, they later gave up an intermediate appeal and abided by the decision of the court.

THE IMPACT OF THE LITIGATION ON NATIONAL POLICY. The 1972 decision of the Tsu local court suggested that neither the emissions control measures embodied in the Air Pollution Control Law (K-value regulation) nor the environmental quality standard for sulfur dioxide were able to protect human health. One year before the court decision, Kakuzo Tanaka, the governor of the Mie Prefecture, had decided to introduce "total emission control." One month after the court decision, the Mie Prefecture Government established "urgent antipollution measures" and asked the factories of the petrochemical complex to reduce their emissions of sulfur oxides. In 1973 total emission control was implemented based on the Mie Prefecture Ordinance for Pollution Control.

This legislation included the following provisions. First, an interim target concentration of 0.025 ppm of sulfur dioxide (annual average) in the ambient air should be met by 1974. Second, a final target concentration of 0.017 ppm (annual average) should be met as soon as possible after the interim target was obtained. Third, fuel consumption at each factory should *not* exceed the amount consumed in 1973. Fourth, the sulfur content of fuel should be regulated below certain levels (0.67 percent to 2.2 percent by 1973, 0.45 percent to 1.5 percent by 1974). Finally, the establishment of new facilities and/or expansion of existing facilities would require permission by the prefecture government. As a result of the introduction of the total emission control measure, annual sulfur oxide emissions from Yokkaichi City declined drastically from over 100,000 tons in 1971 to 17,000 tons in 1975 (ICETT 1992).

When the total emission control was officially introduced by the Prefecture Ordinance, concerns were raised concerning its lawfulness. The Air Pollution Control Law did not permit the local government to establish any regulation of sulfur oxides other than the K-value regulation. Furthermore, the final target of the sulfur dioxide concentration in ambient air of 0.017 ppm was more stringent than the national EQS of 0.05 ppm (annual average). However, based on the experience of Yokkaichi City, the Cabinet amended the national EQS for sulfur dioxide to a standard approximately three times more stringent than the 1973 level. The national government also amended the Air Pollution Control Law in 1974 by including total emission control. These amendments made the local emission control measures of the Mie Prefecture adequate.[16]

A Comparison of the Local Initiatives

Table 2.2 presents the air pollution control measures adopted by the case study cities (Yokohama, Kitakyshu, Osaka, and Yokkaichi) and by Ube City. Citizens' complaints, differing in intensity in each city, proved to be a significant catalyst for environmental management. In Kitakyushu and Yokkaichi, industry was politically influential and economically dominant. The citizens rarely united in collective action; rather they expressed their will through local elections or, as a last resort, through court litigation. In Yokohama and Osaka, citizens were more free from the influence of local industry, and collective actions were taken. In Ube, the pollution control measures occurred in the 1950s when public awareness of the dangers of pollution was much less than in later years.

In Yokohama, Osaka, and Kitakyushu, the mayors played an important role in facilitating pollution control measures. In Yokkaichi, the political will of both the governor and the mayor to arrest pollution was not as evident as in the other three cities. Neither the prefecture nor municipal governments were able to control pollution before the court decision. In Yokkaichi the court deci-

Table 2.2 Air Pollution Control Measures Adopted by Five Local Governments

City	Ube	Yokohama	Osaka	Kitakyushu	Yokkaichi
Period of measure	1950s	mid-1960s	late 1960s and early 1970s	early 1970s	mid-1970s
National law	None	Soot and Smoke Control Law	Soot and Smoke Control Law; later the Air Pollution Control Law	Air Pollution Control Law	Air Pollution Control Law
Local government taking initiative	Municipal government	Municipal government	Municipal government	Municipal government	Prefecture government
Main source of pollution	Large cement factories	A coal-fired power plant and large factories	Small and medium-size industries and building heating facilities	Large factories	A petrochemical complex
Major pollutants	Cement and coal dust	Sulfur oxides	Sulfur oxides and coal dust	Sulfur oxides (coal dust until mid-1960s)	Sulfur oxides
Form of civic protest	Complaints about pollution were submitted to the municipal government; no obvious citizens' movement occurred.	Local medical doctors led intensive movement against air pollution.	Local communities submitted complaints to the municipal government; leftist political parties led antipollution movement.	Citizens supported mayor's rival in the local elections.	Litigation was the catalyst for pollution control measures. No obvious collective action occurred.
Key player or players	A university professor who monitored dust fall	Mayor	Local communities	Local women's associations that conducted studies of pollution	Lawyers ruling in the Tsu Court decision
Administrative instrument	Dust control resolution adopted by municipal assembly	Pollution control agreements (later a municipal ordinance)	Administrative guidance was provided with technical and financial support for SMIs	Pollution control agreements between the municipal government and major polluters	Total emission control (compensation for victims during the 1960s)

Government-industry communication	Meetings between the municipal government and factories	Bargaining between a company and the municipal government when the company establishes and/or expands its production facilities	Meetings where the municipal government explains the necessity of pollution control measures to polluters	Discussions within the Joint Committee on Air Pollution Prevention	No substantive communication seemed to be made before the court decision in 1972
Political stance of the mayor	Conservative	Leftist (Socialist)	Fairly neutral	Conservative	Conservative
Motives of industries to control pollution	To increase production efficiency	To obtain acceptance of local citizens by concluding a pollution control agreement with the municipal government	To preserve feeling of participation in the management of the municipality and to maintain prestige in the local community	To help mayor win re-election	To reduce public criticism
Outcome	The first successful air pollution control measures were adopted before the passage of national legislation.	Japan's first pollution control agreement was concluded.	Successful antipollution measures, particularly for SMIs, were made possible by cooperative relationship between the municipal government and local businesses and by strong administrative capability of the municipal government.	Nippon Steel's initiative facilitated the dialogue between the municipal government and local businesses.	Court decision forced the national government to amend the EQS. Introduction of total emission control by the prefecture government led the national government to follow suit.

Source: Author's summary.

sion was instrumental in changing the policy of the governor on pollution problems. He finally made a strong political commitment to total emission control.

The factors that influenced polluting sources to adopt antipollution measures varied in the five cities. In Ube a cement company recognized the direct economic merit of collecting dust. Polluters in the other cities dealt with public pressure by adopting costly measures to reduce sulfur oxides. Their motivations differed: to establish new facilities in Yokohama, to keep their local prestige in Osaka, and to support their conservative mayor in Kitakyushu. In Yokkaichi, factories in the petrochemical complex undertook antipollution measures after the court decision because of the strong political will of the prefecture governor and growing public pressure.

Solid scientific data played a crucial role in all of the cities. In Ube a university professor monitored dust fall and convinced the factories of the necessity of antipollution measures. In the other three cities, local air pollution problems were scientifically investigated based on accumulated monitoring data using simulation models and costly wind tunnel experiments. By 1965 Yokohama, Kitakyushu, and Osaka had each established a local institute to conduct pollution studies. Clearly, the municipal governments regarded scientific studies as crucial to environmental management. These scientific investigations quantified each polluter's contribution to the local air pollution problem, and the local governments persuaded the polluters to adopt antipollution measures after showing them the results of the investigations.

Conclusion

Japan's sulfur oxide emissions decreased by 82.4 percent from 1970 to 1989. These emissions amounted to 0.5 kilogram per US$1,000 GDP in 1990; in the same year the average of all countries that are members of the Organization for Economic Cooperation and Development was 3.7 kilograms (OECD 1994, 35-36). Japan's timely adjustment in its national policy during the 1970s to include antipollution measures has been aptly described as a "pollution miracle." This adjustment in national policy can be attributed to municipal governments' prior policy changes in response to local citizens' complaints about pollution.

Several factors help explain why pollution in Japan had become so serious: lack of awareness among the local people, industry, and governments; ineffective legislation; and lack of technology and scientific knowledge. As demonstrated by the cities discussed in this chapter, Japan's experience in air pollution control has not been simple but diverse because of cities' differing social and economic backgrounds. Nonetheless, there is no doubt that the Japanese experience can provide useful lessons for developing countries in their efforts to arrest pollution. For example, in cities where small numbers of large factories are the major polluters, similar approaches like that in Yokohama or Kitakyushu, reaching pollution control agreements, may be effective. In cities where small-sized sources are polluting the environment, Osaka's approach may be applicable.

Lastly, the availability of scientific data is very important. All the case cities fully utilized monitoring data and the results of simulations to force factories to adopt anti-pollution measures. They made every effort to collect the data, although it was technically far more difficult to do so during that period than today. In developing countries today, it is a big task to collect and analyze environmental data. By disclosing environmental data, governments can exert pressure to factories and promote public awareness.

Notes

1. Smoke emitted from stacks was also regarded as a symbol of industrialization and economic prosperity in Manchester, England, during the nineteenth century (Bowler and Brimblecombe 2000) and in Pittsburgh, Pennsylvania, in the United States between the late nineteenth and early twentieth centuries (Tarr 1996, 232).

2. Business communities strongly opposed the EQS for sulfur dioxides for the following reasons. First, the standards were more stringent than those established in other industrial nations. Second, vast investments in antipollution measures would be required to attain the standards. Third, procurement of low-sulfur oil became increasingly difficult. Fourth, scientific knowledge at the time was insufficient to establish the EQS (ICETT 1992). As a compromise, the attainment rates stipulated in the draft EQS were amended from 99 percent to 88 percent for hourly values and 70 percent for daily values. Later it became obvious that the standards were unable to prevent adverse health effects (Yoshida 2002).

3. While energy savings investments reduced energy consumption by 4.7 percent, the remaining 5.7 percent reduction was attributed to improvements in operation and management.

4. The OECD reported how Japanese environmental policies are integrated into sector policies (OECD 1994, 95–158).

5. During the 1960s, Mr. Hashimoto, the director of the Pollution Control Division of MHW, was able to meet a director of the Ministry of Construction to discuss environmental issues only after he had visited the office of his counterpart more than ten times.

6. The discussion in this chapter of municipal governments' pollution control measures is primarily based on Fujikura (1998), Osaka (1998), Yoshida (2002), and interviews by the author.

7. The author gratefully acknowledges the helpful information he received from Professor Saruta during several interviews

8. About 40,000 pollution control agreements are still in effect in Japan. Most of the current agreements require factories and other facilities (such as waste incinerators) to meet standards that are much more stringent than national standards. For example, in an agreement the effluent standard for heavy metal is ten times more stringent than the national standard.

9. In 1930 companies along Midosuji Street donated funds for the construction of an underground municipal subway. The main tower of the Osaka Castle was reconstructed in the prewar period with donations from citizens, and a surplus went toward construction of the Osaka Divisional Headquarters of the Imperial Army. Some facilities at the Osaka Port were donated by companies. Because of donations, many municipal elementary schools and kindergartens in Osaka's downtown area have much better facilities than the education facilities in other Japanese municipalities. Finally, donations funded equipment in the city hall and other municipal buildings.

10. In order to avoid this problem, the pollution control agreements concluded in Kitakyushu stipulated that the companies had to adopt new pollution control technologies and that they should make an effort to improve their antipollution measures. The pollution control agreements concluded in Chiba Prefecture during the 1970s were subject to revision every five years in order to catch up with technology development.

11. The discussion of Yokkaichi City is s based primarily on interviews with Professor K. Yoshida and on his report (Yoshida 2002).

12. As early as 1957, fish caught near Yokkaichi began to smell oily, and fish markets refused to buy them. Economic losses reached 79 million yen in 1960, and fishermen demanded that local governments and factories in the complex pay 3 billion yen as compensation. Finally, they agreed on a compensation of 100 million yen, but no measures would be undertaken by factories to treat the effluent.

13. In 1961 the MHW provided a subsidy of one million yen to the municipal government as financial support. In 1969 the national government established the Extraordinary Relief Law for Pollution-Related Health Damage and took over support from the municipal government.

14. During that period, only Tokyo, Kawasaki, Osaka, and Kitakyushu were designated as pollution-controlled areas based on the law.

15. Professor Michio Hashimoto made this statement at a workshop on Practical Environmental Compliance and Enforcement Approaches, held by the World Bank Institute, Kusatsu, Japan, December 9–13, 2002.

16. National "total emission control" has been applied to areas where emission sources are so concentrated that it is deemed difficult to attain the EQS solely with the local emission standards. Prefecture governors determine the total amount of emissions that would be permissible in each area regulated and formulate programs to reduce total emissions. This regulation system has been imposed in twenty-four areas for SOx and eleven areas for NOx.

References

Bowler, C., and P. Brimblecombe. 2000. "Control of Air Pollution in Manchester Prior to the Public Health Act, 1875." *Environmental History* 6: 71–98.

Broadbent, J. 1998. *Environmental Politics in Japan*. Cambridge, England: Cambridge University Press.

Eco Business Network. 1995. *Kankyo* (Environmental) *Business Report*. September 15.

Environment Agency. 1990. *Kankyo Hakusho* (Quality of the Environment in Japan). Tokyo: Okurasho Insatsukyoku.

———. 2001. *Kankyo Hakusho* (Quality of the Environment in Japan). Tokyo: Okurasho Insatsukyoku.

Fujikura, R. 1998. *Dai 3 Sho: Kogaitaisaku No Shakai Keizai Yoin Bunseki* (Chapter 3: Socioeconomic Analysis of Pollution Control Measures. In *Kitakyushushi Kogai Taisakushi Kaiseki Hen* (An Analysis of the History of Pollution Control in Kitakyushu). Kitakyushu Municipal Government.

———. 2001. "A Non-confrontational Approach to Socially Responsible Air Pollution Control: The Electoral Experience of Kitakyushu." *Local Environment*. 6 (4): 469–482.

———. 2002. "Japanese Local Measures for Controlling Sulfur Oxide Emissions: Pollution Control Agreements and Administrative Guidance Adopted during the Era of Rapid Economic Development" (in Japanese). In *Kankyo to Kaihatsu No Seisaku Katei to Dynamism* (Policy Process and Dynamism in Environment and Development), edited by T. Terao and K. Oksuka. Tokyo: Institute for Economic Development.

Fukuoka Prefecture. 1955. *Fukuoka Prefecture Notification*, No. 767. August 20.

Geber, B. 1998. "The Diversity of Environmental Agreements." In *Co-operative Environmental Governance*, edited by P. Glasbergen. Dordrecht: Kluwer Academic Publishers.

Hashimoto, M. 1988. *Shishi Kankyo Gyosei* (My Private History of Environmental Administration). Tokyo: Asahi Shimbun.

Hayashi, E. 1971. *Yahata No Kozai* (Pollution in Yahata). Tokyo: Asahi Shimbun.

Hishida, K. 1974. "Tokyo To Ni Okeru Toshi Kogai No Rekishi" (Urban Pollution in Tokyo Metropolitan Area). In *Kigyo Kankyo* (Industrial Environment) 4(3): 25–67.

ICETT (International Center for Environmental Technology Transfer). 1992. *Yokkaichi Kogai, Kankyo Kaizen No Ayumi* (History of Yokkaichi's Pollution and Environmental Improvement). Yokkaichi.

IES (Institute of Environmental Systems). 1996. *Kankyo Kosuto To Sangyo, Kigyou* (Environmental Expenditure and Industry). IES Report No. 5. Fukuoka: IES of Kyushu University.

IPCS (Institute for Pollution Control Studies of the Tokyo Metropolitan Government). 1970. *Kougai To Toukyoto* (Pollution and Tokyo). Tokyo: Tokyo Metropolitan Government.

ISO World. 2003. http://www.ecology.or.jp/isoworld/iso14000/registr4.htm. January.

Japan Industrial Machinery Association. various years. *Kanyo Sochi Seisan Jisseki Chosa* (Production of Environmental Equipment in Japan). Tokyo.

JEC (Japan Environmental Corporation). 1976. *Kogai Boshi Jigyodan 10 Nen No Ayumi* (A Ten-Year History of the JEC). Tokyo: Gyosei.

Katsuhara, K. 1997. *Chugoku No Kogyoka To Kankyo Mondai* (Chinese Industrialization and Environmental Problems). Notes from a speech on March 18, 1998, at the International Centre for the Study of East Asian Development, Kitakyushu.

Koken Kyokai (Pollution-Related Health Damage Compensation and Prevention Association). 2000. *Nihon No Taiki Osen No Rekishi* (History of Air Pollution in Japan). Tokyo: Koken Kyokai.

Konishi, A. 1996. "Public Lending Schemes for Pollution Control in Japan." *Journal of Development Assistance* 2(1): 137–161.

Kuroda, T. 1996. *Toshi Sangyo Kogai No Genten Nishi-Yodogawa Kogai* (Nishi-Yodogawa; Origin of Urban Industrial Pollution). Tokyo: Doyukan.

Matsumoto, T., et al. 1997. "Japanese-Affiliated Firms and Environmental Problems in China: Environmental Implications of the Foreign Direct Investment." In *Pre-prints of the 5th Symposium on Global Environment*, pp. 299–306. Tokyo: Japan Society of Civil Engineers.

MEIP (The Metropolitan Environment Improvement Program). 1994. *Japan's Experience in Urban Environmental Management*. Washington, D. C.: The World Bank.

MITI (Ministry of International Trade and Industry). various years. *Shuyo Sangyo No Setsubi Toshi Keikaku* (The Investment Plans of Major Industries). Tokyo: Okurasho Insatsukyoku.

Nakayama, H., and H. Imura. 1999. "Regional Characteristics of Industrialization and Pollutant Emission Structures of Chinese Cities." *J. Environmental Systems and Engineering* 636/VII-13: 81–96.

Nose, Y. 1997. Review and Prospects for the Ube-Accommodative Prevention System for Air Pollution in Yamaguchi Prefecture, The Yamaguchi-Ube International Symposium. October.

OECD (Organization for Economic Cooperation and Development). 1994. *OECD Environmental Performance Reviews*. Japan, Paris: OECD.

Osaka. 1998. *Osakashi Kogai Taisakushi* (History of Pollution Control in Osaka City). Osaka Municipal Government, Department of Environment.

Shikata, H. 1991. Kemuri Wo Hoshi Ni Kaeta Machi (A City Turned Smoke into Stars). Tokyo: Kodansha.

Shiroyama, K. 2001. "Hogashi Ajia No Kankyo Seisaku" (Environmental Policy in Eastern Asia). In Ajia No Kankyo Mondai To Shakai Keizai Seido (Environmental Problems and Socioeconomic Systems in Asia), edited by T. Terao and K. Otsuka. Tokyo: Institute of Economic Development.

Shoji, H., and K. Miyamoto. 1964. *Osorubeki Kogai* (Horrible Pollution). Tokyo: Iwanami Shoten.

Terao, T. 1994. "*Nihon No Sangyo Sesaku To Sangyo Kogai*" (Japanese Industrial Policy and Industrial Pollution). In *Kaihatsu To Kankyo* (Development and Environment), edited by R. Kojima and N. Fujisaki, vol. 4. Tokyo: Institute of Development Economics.

Tsuru, S. 1998. "Environmental Problems and Polices in Postwar Japan Reviewed." In *Environmental Economics and Policy Studies* 1: 19–38. Tokyo: Springer-Verlag, Tokyo.

Ube City. 1997. *Creating a City That Harmonizes Environment and Development*. Ube City Municipal Government.

Ui, J. 1989. "Anti-pollution Movements and Other Grass-Roots Organizations." In *Environmental Policy in Japan*, edited by S. Tsuru and Helmut Weidner. Berlin: Edition Sigma.

World Bank. 1995. *World Data 1995*. Washington, D.C.: World Bank.

Yahata Works. 1980. *Yahata Seitetsusho 80 Nen Shi–Bumon Shi Gekan* (An Eighty-Year History of the Yahata Works—A History of the Departments). Kitakyushu: Nippon Steel Corp.

———. 1982. *Enerugi Bu 60 Nen No Ayumi* (A Sixty-Year History of the Energy Division). Kitakyushu: Nippon Steel Corp.

Yoshida, K. 2002. *Yokkaichi Kogai* (Pollution in Yokkaichi). Tokyo: Kashiwa Shobo.

3

Water Management Standards and Environmental Compliance in Japan at the National and Prefectural Levels

Thomas J. Ballatore, Victor S. Muhandiki, and Masahisa Nakamura

The question of how Japan resolved its postwar pollution problems is of great importance to developing countries currently experiencing rapid economic growth. This chapter examines the evolution of water quality standards in Japan and considers how good environmental performance has been promoted.

The first part of the chapter analyzes, at the national level, the Japanese pollution control experience. It reviews the fundamental causes of pollution in postwar Japan and examines the countermeasures and resulting trends in ambient pollution levels. Actions at the subnational level have been the most important in resolving man y environmental problems in Japan. Accordingly, the second part of the chapter focuses on the prefectural level and explores how phosphorus has been controlled at industrial sources in the Lake Biwa watershed in the Shiga Prefecture. Using effluent data from 388 dischargers, this part analyzes why certain firms have reduced their phosphorus discharge. While such a broad analysis is valuable, it leaves specific questions unanswered, such as why an individual discharger or firm makes certain decisions. We turn to this subject in Chapter 4.

Pollution Control at the National Level: An Overview of Japan's Experience

Although environmental problems were not unheard of in Japan before World War II, rapid economic and population growth after the war, along with the concomitant changes in the use of land and resources, put tremendous pressure on the environment. The battle to overcome those problems has been largely successful: Japan's environment is certainly in better shape today than anyone could have imagined in the 1960s. The three main causes of water pollution in postwar Japan—population growth, economic growth (industrialization), and land- and resource-use change—are examined below.

Fundamental Causes of Pollution in Postwar Japan

From 1945 to 1975, Japan's population jumped from 70 million people to 110 million (Ministry of Public Management, Home Affairs, Posts and Telecommunications 2002). Given its relatively small amount of habitable land (only a fifth of Japan's total land area has a slope of less than 10 percent) and an already large population base, Japan in 1945 was the fourth most densely populated country in the world, with 340 persons per square kilometer (United Nations 2000).

In the period from 1955 through 1973, Japan experienced some of the highest economic growth rates in its history. Massive increases in labor productivity, a high domestic savings rate, and a favorable international framework contributed to annual growth in the nation's gross national product (GNP) of more than 10 percent (Tsuru 1993). Unfortunately, in the early postwar period, rapid industrialization also led to a sharp increase in environmental pollution. Interestingly, some signs of pollution, such as black smoke billowing from industries, were a source of pride for many Japanese throughout the 1950s. After the lack of economic activity and high unemployment immediately after the war, the people welcomed the smoke as a sign of industrial progress.

Both economic development and population growth led to a shift from traditional to more consumption-oriented lifestyles. Increases in per capita consumption and waste output, as well as dramatic shifts in resource use, had adverse impacts on the environment. For example, the shift from application of night soil to use of synthetic fertilizers for rice production posed a double source of contamination of rivers and lakes (Ohkubo 2000). First, night soil was not "recycled" but rather was discharged into waterways. Second, runoff of imported synthetic fertilizers into sensitive watersheds affected the water quality of many rivers and lakes. Land-use change, including the loss of wetlands and the increase of impervious surfaces to accommodate more people living more prosperous lives, also negatively affected water quality.

Japan's environmental problems fell into two broad categories: those affecting health and those affecting the productivity of natural resources. Toxic contamination, such as the well-known cases of mercury pollution in Minamata and cadmium pollution in Toyama, led to the injury or death of thousands of people. Additionally, asthma-inducing air pollution occurred in most of Japan's large cities throughout the 1950s and 1960s. These problems and the general deterioration of the environment—as seen in the low dissolved oxygen levels in rivers (for example, the Sumida River) or the devastation of aquatic life in enclosed seas (for example, Dokai Bay)—led to much suffering and public outcry for change and relief.

In short, population and economic growth, along with changes in land and resource use, led to a sharp rise in environmental pollution in postwar Japan. However, as income and living standards rose, so did public discontent with the negative effects of pollution. The mid- to late1960s was a turning point in public consciousness about environmental issues.

Responses to the Pollution Problem

Much has been written about Japan's response to the environmental problems of the postwar era (see, for example, OECD 1977; Aoyama et al. 1993; Cruz et al. 1998; and Okada and Peterson 2000). Therefore, a thorough review of the literature is not attempted here. Instead key factors that led to the dramatic recovery in Japan's environmental conditions are presented.

Clearly, the fundamental response in Japan to pollution was a rise in the general public's consciousness of environmental issues. From this change in thinking came many social, regulatory, and judicial measures to control pollution. Notably, control measures at the local level are of key importance, and their role cannot be underestimated. Although Japan developed at the national level a comprehensive set of environmental laws and regulations in the early 1970s, prior to that period pollution was mainly controlled at the local level through pollution control agreements (PCAs) because the existing national laws and regulations were inadequate.

The first PCA was signed between the city of Yokohama and an electric power company in 1964. The agreement was revolutionary because it specified effluent quality standards without being based on any existing law: the PCA was simply a voluntary agreement between an environmentally active mayor with strong popular support and an industry. Significantly, the strong environmental focus of the PCA was in contrast to the central government's development policy. Because PCAs allowed communities to control pollution locally despite the lack of national government support, they became quite widespread following this first case. Thus, from the first agreement in 1964, the total number of PCAs jumped to approximately 30,000 by the late 1990s (Imura 1998). A key to their effectiveness is the nature of Japanese society and the role of shame and community pressure in influencing polluters' behavior. In Japan dischargers are particularly sensitive about their relations with the community. This is partly because of cultural mores and partly because of the lack of space to relocate businesses. Most importantly, workers usually live nearby and can be ostracized by the community for any real or apparent threats posed by the companies they work for. While there are no legal penalties for violation of a PCA, the threat of a damaged reputation provided enough incentive for compliance.

The dramatic shift in mainstream views concerning the relative importance of environmental protection versus economic growth was codified in a set of environmental laws passed by the "Pollution Session" of the Japanese Diet in 1970. The Water Pollution Control Law of 1970 greatly strengthened the scope and level of national effluent standards. Table 3.1 presents the ambient standards and effluent standards for health-related items (toxics), and the effluent standards for living environment-related items (nontoxics) are given in Table 3.2. The law also gave authority to local governments to set stricter standards when necessary due to local conditions. In the case of the Shiga Prefecture, these local standards have played a major role in controlling pollution in Lake Biwa.

Trends in Water Quality

The responses outlined above have had a dramatic effect on discharges of regulated toxic pollutants from industries. Nonconformity with ambient standards had fallen to well below 0.1 percent

Table 3.1 *National Ambient and Effluent Standards for Toxic Pollutants in Japan*

Toxic pollutant	Ambient standard	Effluent standard	Year of enactment (most recent revision)
Cadmium	0.01	0.1	1970
Total cyanide	0.01	1	1970
Organic phosphorus	Discontinued	1	1970 (1972)
Lead	0.01	0.1	1970 (1993)
Hexavalent chromium	0.05	0.5	1970
Arsenic	0.01	0.1	1970 (1993)
Total mercury	0.0005	0.005	1970 (1974)
Alkyl mercury	ND	ND	1970 (1974)
PCB	ND	0.003	1975
Dichloromethane	0.02	0.2	1993
Tetrachloroethylene	0.002	0.02	1993
1,2-dichloroethane	0.004	0.04	1993
1,1-dichloroethylene	0.02	0.2	1993
cis-1,2-dichloroethylene	0.04	0.4	1993
1,1,1-trichloroethane	1	3	1993
1,1,2-trichloroethane	0.006	0.06	1993
Trichloroethylene	0.03	0.3	1993
Tetrachloroethylene	0.01	0.1	1993
1,3-dichloropropene	0.002	0.02	1993
Thiram	0.006	0.06	1993
Simazine	0.003	0.03	1993
Thiobencarb	0.02	0.2	1993
Benzene	0.01	0.1	1993
Selenium	0.01	0.1	1993

ND Not detectable.
Note: Units are in milligrams per liter.
Source: Ministry of Environment (2000).

Table 3.2 *National Effluent Standards for Nontoxic Pollutants in Japan*

Pollutant	Standard	Year of enactment (most recent revision)
pH (discharge into coastal areas)	5.0 to 8.6	1970
pH (discharge into other water bodies)	5.8 to 8.6	1970
BOD (rivers)	160 (daily average, 120)	1970
COD (lakes and coastal areas)	160 (daily average, 120)	1970
SS	200 (daily average, 120)	1970
n-Hexane extracts (coastal areas)	5.0	1970
Total coliforms (rivers and lakes)	Daily average of 3,000/cm^3	1970
Total nitrogen	120 (daily average, 60)	1982 for lakes, 1991 for coastal areas
Total phosphorus	16 (daily average, 8)	1982 for lakes, 1991 for coastal areas

Note: Maximum values are in milligrams per liter unless indicated.
Source: Ministry of Environment (2000).

for most toxic substances by 1992 (see Figure 3.1). The sudden increase in 1993 of nonconformity is because of the addition of new substances to the regulated list (see Table 3.1) and the tightening of standards for other substances. Therefore, the data in Figure 3.1 before and after 1992 should be analyzed separately. While the general drop in nonconformity from 1971 to 1992 is significant, many toxic substances discharged into the environment are not on the list of regulated pollutants

Figure 3.1 *Nonconformity with Ambient Standards for Toxic Pollutants, 1970–2000*

Percent of nonconforming companies

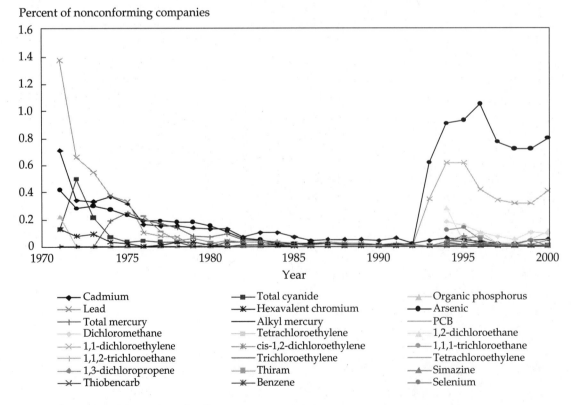

Source: Ministry of Environment (2000).

Figure 3.2 *Conformity with Ambient Standards for BOD/COD, 1970–2000*

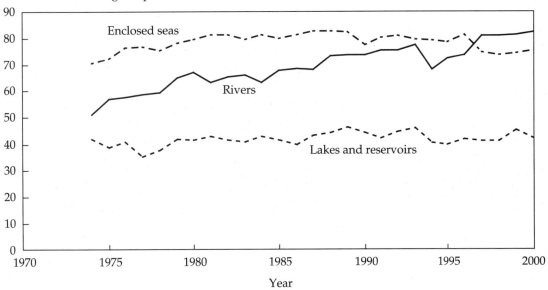

Percent of conforming companies

Source: Ministry of Environment (2000).

and have no ambient standard. The current list is disproportionately composed of substances that have at one time or another caused serious problems in Japan. Nevertheless, Japan's success in reducing the concentrations of the toxic substances shown in Figure 3.1 is noteworthy.

Japan had less success in dealing with nontoxic or organic pollutants. Conformity with ambient standards for biological oxygen demand (BOD) or chemical oxygen demand (COD) did not significantly improve between 1970 and 2000 (see Figure 3.2). Notably, the pollution rates for lakes and reservoirs stayed fairly constant. This indicates that the responses outlined above were not sufficient to halt the deteriorating quality of many of Japan's water bodies.

Summary

Although environmental problems remain in Japan today, the nation's handling of the pollution crisis that developed after World War II can be praised as a success. Interestingly, the causes of the environmental problems and the solutions to them had similar roots. The environmental problems were caused by the economic and social developments that took place in Japan after the war. That is, socioeconomic developments led to pollution problems; they also led to an aversion to pollution by the general public and its desire to tackle the problems by any means. In Japan this shift in thinking was first demonstrated at the local level through pollution control agreements and lawsuits only to be later augmented by formal laws and regulations.

Pollution Control at the Prefectural Level: The Case of Phosphorus Pollution in the Shiga Prefecture

The Shiga Prefecture, located in central Japan and surrounding Lake Biwa, has been relatively progressive in combating environmental pollution. The importance of Lake Biwa to the economy and culture of the area helps explain the greater value given to the environment in Shiga than in some other places in Japan. This section examines the evolution of environmental policies in

Shiga, particularly those policies related to phosphorus, which is the limiting nutrient in Lake Biwa's eutrophication. Ambient and effluent standards for phosphorus in the Lake Biwa watershed are discussed as well as the legal bases for those standards and the rationale behind them. In addition, monitoring and enforcement are described. Compliance rates are based on raw data from monitoring and published government statistics on regulatory actions for noncompliance. Finally, nonregulatory constraints on dischargers' behavior are examined in order to explain why so many dischargers are well below their allowed effluent concentrations.

Ambient Standards

The Basic Environmental Law sets ambient standards to (1) protect human health from toxic chemicals and (2) preserve the living environment by reducing nontoxic pollutants such as COD, nitrogen, and phosphorus. Standards to preserve the environment are called environmental quality standards (EQSs), and they have a legal basis in Article 16 of the Basic Environmental Law. Paragraph 1 states that the national government (Ministry of Environment) shall establish ambient standards for the protection of the living environment for different classes of water bodies. Paragraph 2 states that the national government may delegate the authority to designate the class of a water body to the prefectural governor by means of a Cabinet Order. However, for major water bodies like Lake Biwa, the national government directly sets the class level, partially to discourage prefectures from competing to attract or keep dischargers by implementing weak standards. Although EQSs are goals that are not legally binding, they serve an important role as a basis for setting effluent standards.

Lake Biwa is classified as Class AA for nontoxic pollutants such as pH, COD, suspended solids (SS), dissolved oxygen (DO), and fecal coliforms. It is classified as Class II for nitrogen and phosphorus; the ambient concentration of phosphorus must be below 0.01 milligrams per liter (mg/L), and nitrogen must be below 0.1 mg/L. The EQSs for nitrogen and phosphorus were added following the Lake Law of 1984. Recognizing the difficulty of quickly meeting the phosphorus EQS for the Southern Basin, the Environment Agency set a target of 0.012 mg/L in 1985 to be met as soon as possible. However, compliance has not yet been attained, nor does it appear imminent. The phosphorus level in the Northern Basin has been below 0.01 mg/L since 1980, yet algal blooms and other signs of eutrophication continue to occur. This suggests that the EQS for phosphorus may be inadequate.

Effluent Standards

In order to meet the ambient standards, effluent standards have been developed and implemented at the national and prefectural levels for control of industrial and municipal point sources. In addition, Shiga has undertaken other important measures. For example, it has banned phosphorus-containing detergents, extended the collection area of the sewerage system, and reintroduced the natural reed beds surrounding the lake. The national effluent standards, however, have been significant in reducing the pollution load entering the lake.

NATIONAL CONCENTRATION-BASED EFFLUENT STANDARDS. The Water Pollution Control Law of 1970 is the statutory basis for national effluent standards. It should be noted that these standards are concentration based. The authority to make load-based standards is given by the Lake Law of 1984.

Article 3, Paragraph 1, of the Water Pollution Control Law states that "the effluent standards regarding the extent of pollution . . . shall be established by Ordinance of the Prime Minister's Office." Paragraph 2 requires that the standards be the maximum permissible amount (load) for health-related items (that is, for toxic pollutants) and the maximum permissible level (concentration) for items related to the living environment (that is, for nontoxic pollutants such as phosphorus). Article 2, Paragraph 2, of the law designates "Specified Facilities" that are the targets of regulation to be determined by Cabinet Order.

The standards for phosphorus are for the daily maximum less than 16 mg/L and for the daily average less than 8 mg/L.] These levels are designed to provide the minimum level of environmental protection: they must be met by specified facilities anywhere in the nation. National uniform standards discourage prefectures from setting weaker effluent standards to attract dischargers. Prefectures that must protect sensitive resources (for example, the Lake Biwa watershed in the Shiga Prefecture) need standards that are stricter than the national standards.

PREFECTURAL CONCENTRATION-BASED EFFLUENT STANDARDS. As noted earlier, the national uniform effluent standards provide a minimum level of environmental protection. For prefectures like Shiga that have resources that are heavily dependent upon environmental factors, these standards are inadequate. Therefore, the Water Pollution Control Law authorizes prefectural governors to set stricter standards.

Article 3, Paragraph 3, states that "when there is any Public Water Area under prefectural jurisdiction for which the effluent standards as established under Paragraph 1 are recognized to be insufficient for…protecting the living environment, the Prefecture may establish more stringent standards than the maximum permissible levels stipulated . . . by enacting Prefectural Ordinances in accordance with criteria to be stipulated by Cabinet Order." Shiga determined the national standards to be insufficient and passed prefectural standards first in 1972 on COD and then in 1979 on nitrogen and phosphorus.

Under the authority of Article 3.3 of the Water Pollution Control Law, Shiga implemented a prefectural ordinance in 1972 that set stricter levels on COD, BOD, and SS discharges from specified facilities. At that time the Water Pollution Control Law did not specify nitrogen or phosphorus as items to be regulated, so they were left out of the 1972 ordinance. By the late 1970s, eutrophication symptoms (like algal blooms, loss of transparency, excessive weed growth, and taste and odor problems in the water supply) had become increasingly obvious. Control of COD alone was not enough; nutrient control was also necessary. In 1979 Shiga passed the Eutrophication Prevention Ordinance (EPO), this time including nitrogen and phosphorus. This practice of including nonspecified items in prefectural ordinances became known as *yokodashi* (roughly translated as "added on the side"). It was quite revolutionary at the time, reflecting as it did a major increase in local autonomy. The same practice was followed later by Shiga to extend the range of regulated dischargers to include flow rates below 50 cubic meters per day (m³/day).

Concentration-based effluent standards for phosphorus are shown in Table 3.3. The levels are maximum allowable concentrations. In 1997 new standards for companies discharging between 10 and 30 m³/day were added, but monitoring data were not available for this study.

In general, standards are established through the following process. An issue comes up and is recommended by the Environmental Policy Section of the prefectural government to the head of the Environmental Bureau. Under the authority of the governor, the head of the Environment Bureau refers the issue to the Prefectural Environmental Council. The council is made up of Assembly members, professors, business leaders, and other concerned parties. The council makes recommendations on effluent levels, for example, to the governor, who can then recommend the proposal to the Prefectural Assembly, which has the final vote on whether or not to pass the ordinance (Kagatsume 1998).

In the case of Shiga's Eutrophication Prevention Ordinance of 1979, debate among the council members concerning the standards in Table 3.3 was contentious (Fukada 1984). The standards were based on criteria shown in Table 3.4. It was assumed that all dischargers—except food

Table 3.3 *Concentration-Based Effluent Standards for Industries in Shiga, Japan*

Type of industry	Flow rate in cubic meters per day	Total pollution (milligrams per liter) for existing sources	Total pollution (milligrams per liter) for new sources
Food	30–50	4	2
	50–1,000	3	1.5
	1,000~	2	1
Lunch box	30–50	5	4
	50–1,000	5	3
	1,000~	3	2
Textile	30–50	2	1.2
	50–1,000	1.5	0.8
	1,000~	1	0.5
Chemical	30–50	2	1.2
	50–1,000	1.5	0.8
	1000~	1	0.5
Gelatin	30–50	2	1.2
	50–1,000	1.5	0.8
	1,000~	1	0.5
Other	30–50	1.5	1
	50–1,000	1.2	0.6
	1,000~	0.8	0.5

Source: Shiga Prefectural Government (1998).

industries—could achieve a phosphorus effluent of 1 milligram per liter in their process water by using the coagulation-sedimentation process. The standards take into account that different types of manufacturers use different ratios of cooling and mixing water to dilute effluents. For food industries it was assumed that biological treatment would be used, but food industries could not achieve the same consistent removals as coagulation-sedimentation, so for them less strict standards were set (Oka 1997).

PREFECTURAL LOAD-BASED EFFLUENT STANDARDS. As mentioned earlier, the Water Pollution Control Law of 1970 only gives the authority to set concentration-based standards for living environment–related pollutants like phosphorus. For a long time, the prefectural government

Table 3.4 *Criteria for Phosphorus Standards*

Standard	Phosphorus concentration in milligrams per liter by industry type			
	Food	Textiles	Chemicals	Others
Raw process water	5	10	5	10.5
Treated process water	1	1	1	1
Total wastewater [P]	0.97	0.83	0.8	0.94
Standard (average)	2	1	1	0.8
Standard (maximum)	3	1.5	1.5	1.2

Note: The standards shown are for industries with flow rates between 50 and 1,000 cubic meters per day. The standards are approximately 30 percent looser for flows between 30 and 50 cubic meters per day and 30 percent tighter for flows more than 1,000 cubic meters per day.

Source: Oka (1995).

preferred the concentration-based standards to the load-based standards because concentration-based standards would not interfere with the competing goal of economic expansion of existing firms. However, problems like eutrophication are related to load, not concentration, of nutrients. The need for a statutory basis for load-based standards to control eutrophication was recognized and codified in the Lake Law of 1984 (which was modeled on Shiga's EPO of 1979). The prefectures were given the authority to set load-based regulations for specified facilities. However, it was not until 1996 that load-based standards were set in Shiga. The levels for new sources are shown in Table 3.5. The targeted dischargers have flow rates of 50 m³/day and over. New dischargers must meet a standard of

$$\text{Load} = a\text{Flow}^b \times 10^{-3}$$

where load is in kilograms per day and flow is in cubic meters per day. Existing dischargers are given a slight break. Nonetheless, the a and b coefficients were set so as to mirror the concentration-based standards.

Monitoring and Enforcement

Spot inspections and self-monitoring are the main ways in which effluent quality are monitored in the Shiga Prefecture and throughout Japan. In Shiga the seven district offices are in charge of monitoring and enforcing effluent regulations for dischargers within their districts; they are also in charge of determining who is complying and setting penalties for noncompliance. The central prefectural office compiles data and publishes summaries in its annual White Paper on the Environment, but it does not make enforcement decisions.

SPOT INSPECTIONS. Article 25 gives the governor the authority to conduct unannounced inspections of regulated dischargers. The cost of these inspections is borne by the government. Budget and human resource limitations mean that inspections are usually carried out on a yearly basis (Shichiri 1998). Roughly 4 percent of inspections take place at night, and all are unannounced (Ishiguro 1998). The inspector must present appropriate identification, and the law specifically states that such inspections shall in no way be construed as part of a criminal investigation. Water samples are taken and sent to an analysis company chosen yearly by the prefecture based on a

Table 3.5 Load-Based Standards for Phosphorus

Type of industry	Flow rate in cubic meters per day	a coefficient	b coefficient
Food	50–1,000	1.93	0.94
	1,000~	1.54	0.94
Lunch box	50–1,000	3.85	0.94
	1,000~	3.08	0.94
Textile	50–1,000	0.91	0.97
	1,000~	0.62	0.97
Chemical	50–1,000	0.91	0.97
	1,000~	0.62	0.97
Gelatin	50–1,000	0.91	0.97
	1,000~	0.62	0.97
Other	50–1,000	0.71	0.96
	1,000~	0.67	0.96

Source: Shiga Prefectural Government (1998).

competitive bid (Kagatsume 1998). Samples are tested for all the regulated items including phosphorus. The flow rate given in the discharger's operating permit is accepted unless visual inspection reveals any significant irregularities. Flow rates that appear to be significantly higher than in the operating permit will be directly measured (Shichiri 1998).

Figures 3.3, 3.4, and 3.5 present spot inspection results for 1995 for manufacturing sources over 30 m³/day (388 dischargers). The degree of compliance with the concentration-based standards for phosphorus described in Table 3.3 is shown. The regulations in Table 3.3 cover six industry types; the results can be shown in only three figures because (a) the lunch box industry is combined with the food industry in the inspection result summary and (b) the textile, chemical, and gelatin industries all have the same standards for the targeted flow rates of over 30 m³/day.

Note that the x-axes in Figures 3.4 and 3.5 are drawn on a logarithmic scale because of the presence of some dischargers with very large flows; for the food industry (Figure 3.3), the maximum discharge is only 1,200 m³/day. New sources were not differentiated in the spot inspection data so it is not clear which dischargers face the stricter "new source" standards. Overall, spot inspections tend to show high rates of compliance. Out of 388 dischargers, there are about 30 violators (indicated by the points that lie above the regulation line in Figures 3.3, 3.4, and 3.5). For the food industry, the three points above the line from 100 to 300 m³/day may not indicate violations because they may be for lunch box industries. All other points above the line in the three figures show violations. Some points below the lines in the figures could indicate a violation if they are new sources facing stricter regulations than existing ones; however, this is impossible to determine given the available data. According to the prefectural government, only 10 to 20 percent of the sources in Shiga are considered "new" (Kagatsume 1998). Dischargers that have expanded operations are considered "existing sources." Unfortunately, information on which dischargers are considered existing and which ones are considered new is not available.

SELF-MONITORING. Article 27 of the Eutrophication Prevention Ordinance requires that specified facilities measure the condition of their effluents at intervals given in the ordinance's enforcement regulations. Article 12, Paragraph 1, states that measurements of phosphorus, nitrogen, and flow rate must be taken by standard methods at least once a month. Paragraph 2 requires that the

Figure 3.3 *Spot Inspection Results for Food Industries*

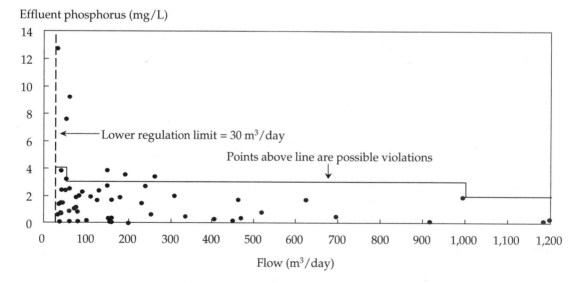

Note: The number of companies is 55; the number of possible violations is 7.
Source: Shiga Prefectural Government (1998).

Figure 3.4 *Spot Inspection Results for Textile and Chemical Industries*

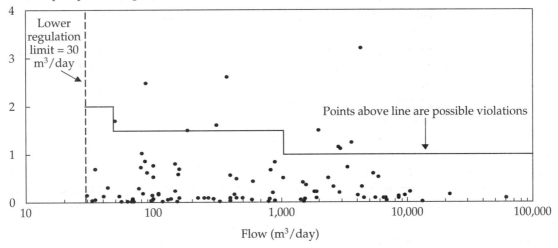

Effluent phosphorus (mg/L)

Note: The number of companies is 93; the number of possible violations is 8.
Source: Shiga Prefectural Government (1998).

records be preserved for three years, but it prohibits the government from officially recording them. For self-inspections, samples must be taken by a licensed person within the discharging firm, and they must be tested at private analysis companies; therefore, the prefectural government assumes that the self-monitoring results are not biased.

RATES OF COMPLIANCE AND NONCOMPLIANCE. Although the great majority of dischargers have phosphorus effluent concentrations below required levels (see Figures 3.3, 3.4, and 3.5), some are over the limit, and enforcement actions in cases of noncompliance are the responsibility of the

Figure 3.5 *Spot Inspection Results for Other Industries*

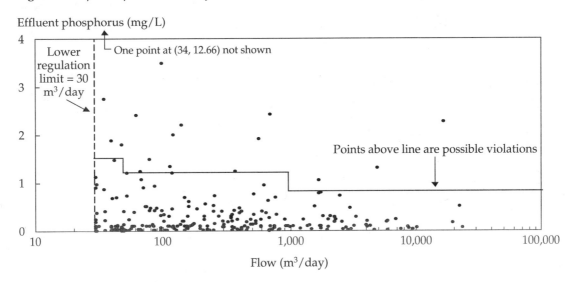

Effluent phosphorus (mg/L)

Note: The number of companies is 240; the number of possible violations is 15.
Source: Shiga Prefectural Government (1998).

environmental bureaus in the local prefectural offices. The number and type of administrative actions taken in 1997 for nitrogen and phosphorus violations are shown in Table 3.6.

Shichiri (1998) estimates that phosphorus violations account for approximately 40 percent of the dischargers indicated as noncompliant in Table 3.6. In this table the data are for all "enterprises (*jigyousho*)" with flow rates greater than 10 m³/day. The enterprises include many dischargers, including animal waste treatment centers and hotels, which tend to have more violations than manufacturers. A relatively high percentage of violations can be expected in the group of manufacturers with flows less than 30 m³/day because they were not regulated until 1997. In conclusion, phosphorus violations exist for the group of manufacturers over 30 m³/day, but they are a mere handful a year (Ishiguro 1998).

Yet Figures 3.3, 3.4, and 3.5 show more than a handful of annual violations. Why is there a discrepancy? It may be that the government is reluctant to find noncompliance based only on the spot inspection results. Reportedly, there is a written administrative procedure for determining compliance and steps to take for noncompliance, but it is not public information. However, Fukada (1998) has shed some light on the process. If the results of the spot inspection reveal a violation of the standard, the regulators and the suspected violator meet, and the discharger has an opportunity to explain the reasons for noncompliance. The self-monitoring data may be used in this case to explain that the spot inspection data are nonrepresentative. If the violation is minor, a "light warning" is issued. If the violation is serious, a strong warning is issued along with suggestions for process improvements. These two administrative actions are not based on any legal authority and are, therefore, nonbinding. In Japan, however, such "administrative guidance" is usually heeded by companies. If the warnings are ignored for several years (for nontoxic items like phosphorus), then "administrative measures" based on the authority given in the Eutrophication Prevention Ordinance are taken. An improvement order is given, and if ignored, a stoppage order is issued. This rarely happens for phosphorus discharge violations.

NONREGULATORY CONSTRAINTS ON DISCHARGERS' BEHAVIOR. Why are most of the dischargers well below their allowed phosphorus concentrations (see Figures 3.3, 3.4, and 3.5)? Following are several possible reasons:

- Because of variability in process efficiency, dischargers include a safety factor in their abatement processes in order to meet the maximum concentration level.
- Some dischargers, because of the nature of their industry, do not produce large amounts of phosphorus effluent.

Table 3.6 *Compliance with Phosphorus and Nitrogen Effluent Standards, 1997*

Item		*Flow over 50 cubic meters per day*	*Flow between 10 and 50 cubic meters per day*
Number of inspected dischargers		939	409
Number not in compliance		41	9
Administrative actions			
"Measures"	*Stoppage Order*	0	0
	Improvement Order	0	0
"Guidance"	*Strong Warning*	17	3
	Light Warning	21	9

Note: More than one administrative action can be taken against a noncompliant discharger.
Source: Shiga Prefectural Government (1998).

- Some dischargers have bought equipment that provides overcontrol.
- Some dischargers have planned ahead and made larger than necessary investments in equipment, thereby achieving better abatement than permitted effluent levels.
- Effluent levels specified in pollution control agreements may be stricter than Shiga's standards (discussed below).
- Companies with ISO 14001 certification are continually trying to minimize their environmental impact (discussed below).
- Some companies feel a sense of good will and voluntarily reduce their effluent levels without outside pressure.

Figure 3.6 shows a hypothetical example of monthly self-inspection results for a typical food industry with a flow rate of 50 m³/day. Both legal and extralegal constraints that influence the industry's effluent levels are shown. The national standards will not be binding for companies in Shiga. In addition, there may be a pollution control agreement that is stricter than the prefectural standard. (These issues are explored in detail in Chapter 4.)

POLLUTION CONTROL AGREEMENTS. Pollution control agreements made in a mayor's office between dischargers and local citizens are a unique characteristic of environmental policy in Japan and an effective means of reducing pollution. PCAs for water pollution in Shiga exist between many large dischargers and local citizens. Because these agreements came after the environmental laws and regulations, their importance is less than the agreements of the 1960s, but they do contain some interesting provisions. The mayor's office in Otsu, the largest city in Shiga, has eighteen pollution control agreements on record and approximately half of them include phosphorus as an item. There are explicit load-based and concentration-based levels incorporated into the agreements. Shiga did not implement load-based standards until 1996, so the load-based levels in the PCAs for major dischargers were a way of balancing the goal of environmental protection with the goal of economic growth of existing firms in the prefecture.

ISO 14001. Certification of environmental management systems, such as ISO 14001, is proceeding rapidly in Japan.[1] The Shiga Prefecture is leading the country in the percentage of

Figure 3.6 Legal and Extralegal Constraints on Discharge

Effluent phosphorus (mg/l)

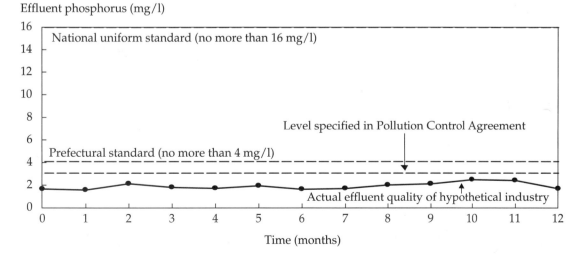

Time (months)

Source: Authors' hypothetical food industry case.

dischargers certified. While ISO 14001 does not specify a specific effluent quality, it does require a member to implement an environmental management system. This means that the impacts of corporate activities on the environment must be assessed and actions taken to continually minimize such impacts (Whitelaw 1997). Overall, the impact of ISO 14001 on effluent quality is positive, but dischargers receiving certification are usually large exporters with already low phosphorus effluent concentrations. The interaction of ISO 14001 with formal regulations and pollution control agreements is not clear.

Conclusion

This chapter has underscored the importance of social pressure in convincing dischargers to control pollution. Although the environmental laws and regulations of Japan have certainly had a positive effect on effluent quality, the gains in pollution abatement would have been far less in the cases examined if it were not for the strong social pressure on polluters to make them address the problems they created.

Because local government authorities have the most immediate responsibility for environmental management at the local level, their capacity (institutional, technical, and financial) must be developed. Local authorities should have legal powers to implement and enforce environmental laws. It is also necessary to develop support mechanisms at the local level through which victims of environmental pollution can seek redress. Victims need assistance from persons with scientific and legal expertise.

Today many developing countries are faced with the challenge of harmonizing the dual goals of development and environmental conservation. The lessons learned from Japan's experience—namely that public awareness and public participation are essential in the resolution of environmental problems—can be of real value to developing countries in their own pollution control efforts.

Note

1. ISO is the name of the International Organization for Standardization. Because the name would have different abbreviations in different languages (for example, IOS in English, OIN in French for Organisation internationale de normalization), the founding countries decided to use a word derived from the Greek isos, meaning "equal."

The ISO 14000 set of standards is primarily concerned with "environmental management." This term refers to what the organization does to minimize the harmful effects on the environment caused by its activities and to achieve continual improvement of its environmental performance.

There are other sets of standards. For example, the ISO 9000 family is primarily concerned with "quality management." This term refers to what the organization does to fulfill the customer's quality requirements and applicable regulatory requirements, while enhancing customer satisfaction and achieving continual improvement of its performance in pursuit of these objectives.

References

Aoyama, Shunsuke, et al. 1993. *Japan's Experience in Urban Environmental Management*. Washington, D.C.: World Bank.

Cruz, Wilfrido, Kazuhiko Takemoto, and Jeremy Warford, eds. 1998. *Urban and Industrial Management in Developing Countries: Lessons from the Japanese Experience*. EDI Learning Resources Series. Washington, D.C.: World Bank.

Fukada, Fumio. 1984. "Lake Biwa's Problems and Shiga's Ordinance (*Biwako mondai to Shigaken jorei*)." In *Ordinances for Lake Water Quality Protection* (*Kosho shuishitsu hozen jorei*), edited by Masashi Kaneko and Tetsuo Seki. Tokyo: Hokki Publishers.

————. 1998. Telephone interview on 15 December.

Imura, Hidefumi. 1998. *The Use of Voluntary Approaches in Japan: An Initial Survey*. OECD: Paris.

Ishiguro, Minoru. 1998. Personal interview on 15 December.

Kagatsume, Toshiaki. 1998. Personal interview on 15 December.

Matsui, S. 1993. "Pollution Control in Japan: A Historical Perspective." In *Environmental Pollution Control: The Japanese Experience*. Papers presented at the United Nations University International Symposium on Eco-Restructuring, 5–7 July 1993, Tokyo, Japan.

Ministry of Environment (Japan). 2000. *White Paper on the Environment (in Japanese)*. Tokyo.

Ministry of Public Management, Home Affairs, Posts and Telecommunications (Japan). 2002. http://www.stat.go.jp/english/data/kokusei/2000/kihon1/00/01.htm Accessed on April 28.

OECD (Organization for Economic Cooperation and Development). 1977. *Environmental Policies in Japan*. Paris.

Ohkubo, Takuya. 2000. "Lake Biwa." In *Water Pollution Control Policy and Management: The Japanese Experience*, edited by M. Okada and S. Peterson. Tokyo: Gyosei.

Oka, Toshihiro. 1995. "Command and Control Approach for Water Pollution Control in Japan: The Experience of Lake Biwa Nutrient Control." In *Proceedings from Environmental Economics Forum on Lake Biwa Eutrophication Control*. Shiga: Lake Biwa Research Institute.

————. 1997. "Direct Regulation (*Chokusetsu kisei*)." In *The Economics of Environmental Policy* (*Kankyo seisaku no keizaigaku*), edited by Kazuhiro Ueta et al. Tokyo: Nihon Hyoronsha.

Okada, M., and S. Peterson, eds. 2000. *Water Pollution Control Policy and Management: The Japanese Experience*. Tokyo: Gyosei..

Shichiri, Shoichi. 1998. Personal interview on 15 December.

Shiga Prefectural Government. 1998. *White Paper on Environment (in Japanese)*. Otsu, Japan.

Tsuru, Shigeto. 1993. *Japan's Capitalism: Creative Defeat and Beyond*. Cambridge, England: Cambridge University Press..

United Nations. 2000. *World Population Prospects*. New York.

Whitelaw, Ken. 1997. *ISO 14001 Environmental System Handbook*. Oxford: Butterworth-Heinemann.

4

Local Efforts to Control Water Pollution: Case Study of a Metal-Plating Industry in the Shiga Prefecture

Victor S. Muhandiki, Thomas J. Ballatore, and Masahisa Nakamura

In Chapter 3 we examined reasons for the compliance of numerous dischargers in the Shiga Prefecture with phosphorus effluent regulations. This chapter focuses on an individual company, RK Excel, and explores how this metal-plating firm in Shiga has managed its effluent quality since the start of its plating operations in 1951. Surprisingly, formal laws and regulations appear to have been less important in inducing good environmental performance by the firm than community pressure. Indeed, the most important factor influencing RK Excel's decisions to lower the concentration of pollutants it discharges into the environment has been community pressure, within the context of changing environmental values throughout Japan and expanding markets for pollution control equipment. Finally, the chapter examines the company's chromium contamination of groundwater and how pollution accidents are handled in Japan.[1]

Taken in proper context, Japan's experience with controlling pollution holds many valuable lessons, particularly for countries currently struggling with the perceived "growth versus environment" dilemma. Those lessons are summarized in the conclusion of this chapter.

The History of Pollution Control at RK Excel

RK Excel Co., Ltd., is a metal-plating company that produces automobile and motorcycle parts. The current company was founded in 1989 as a result of a merger between Takasago Chain Co., Ltd., and Takasago Manufacturing Co., Ltd. The company has its head office in Tokyo, and it has two factories: one in the Shiga Prefecture (located in the town of Yagura, Kusatsu City) and the other in the Saitama Prefecture. The Shiga factory, which is the subject of this chapter and is referred to here as RK Excel, has been in operation since 1943. RK Excel mainly produces motorcycle rims and automobile wheels. It employs 123 persons, has an annual operating capital of 4.24 billion yen, and holds 60 percent of the world's market share in rims.

The company uses chromium in its metal-plating operations. The main toxic substance of concern is hexavalent chromium (Cr^{6+}). If released into the environment and ingested, it has severe toxic and carcinogenic effects. RK Excel also uses and discharges less toxic metals such as reduced chromium (Cr^{3+}), copper, and nickel. Variable pH that results from both production and pollution control methods is another major concern. Table 4.1 shows a complete list of pollutants for which RK Excel is being regulated.

We thank Akira Yamamoto of RK Excel Co., Ltd., for providing extensive information for this case study. We also thank him for facilitating site visits at the factory.

Table 4.1 *RK Excel's Wastewater Quality and Effluent Standards*

	Water quality		Effluent standard			
Symbol	Pre-treatment	Post-treatment	National (1970)	Prefectural (1972)	Municipal (1978)	Neighborhood (1976)
COD	77.8	4.71	160	50	50	30
SS	3.62	0.58	200	70	70	30
Oil	1.00	1.05	5	5	5	3
Fe^{3+}	6.45	0.58	10	10	10	10
Cu^{2+}	1.8	0.103	3	1	1	0.1
Ni^{2+}	95	0.217	NA	NA	1	1
T-Cr	12.5	0.0092	2	0.1	0.1	0.1
Cr^{6+}	12.5	ND	0.5	0.05	0.05	0.05
CN	0.0015	0.0002	1	0.1	0.1	NA
pH	3.0	7.0	5.8 to 8.6	6.0 to 8.5	6.0 to 8.5	6.0 to 8.0

NA Not applicable (no standard exists).
ND Not detectable below 0.001 mg/l.
Note: All figures in mg/l.
Source: Unpublished data from RK Excel.

Since the start of its plating operations in 1951, RK Excel has implemented various methods to control its effluent quality. For the period from 1951 to 1970, there was no legal requirement to abate pollution, yet the company took pollution control actions. Therefore, nonregulatory factors must be considered as well as regulations when explaining RK Excel's pollution abatement decisions.

The basic methods used by RK Excel to control the quality of its effluent have not changed since 1951:

1. Reduction of Cr^{6+} to Cr^{3+}
2. Coagulation-sedimentation
3. pH neutralization.

What have changed are the *extent* and *quality* of these methods over time. It is possible to divide pollution control at RK Excel into four phases: 1951–58, 1959–69, 1970–72, and 1973–present. Each phase and the reasons behind the efforts to control pollution are explored below. Figures 4.1 and 4.2 give an overview of the control methods used in each phase.

Phase 1: 1951 to 1958

Although there were no formal environmental regulations during Phase 1 from 1951 to 1958, RK Excel nevertheless carried out pollution control activities. Their main purpose was lowering the discharge of Cr^{6+}. Its toxic effects were well known at the time, and it would have been unthinkable for the company to allow raw discharge of hexavalent chromium into the environment. In this early period, RK Excel used simple earthen pits as reactors for each pollution control process. These pits may seem primitive by today's standards, but they were commonly used at the time. The pits were lined with what the company thought was clay but what turned out to be a more porous soil. Seepage of pollutants from the pits into the soil and groundwater was possible, yet it was never discovered, and there were no complaints from the local community. Through this system, RK Excel controlled its Cr^{6+} effluent. It is assumed here that the other pollutants indicated in Figure 4.1 were also reduced, although no data exist to confirm this.

Figure 4.1 *Phases 1 through 3 of Pollution Control at RK Excel (1951 to 1972)*

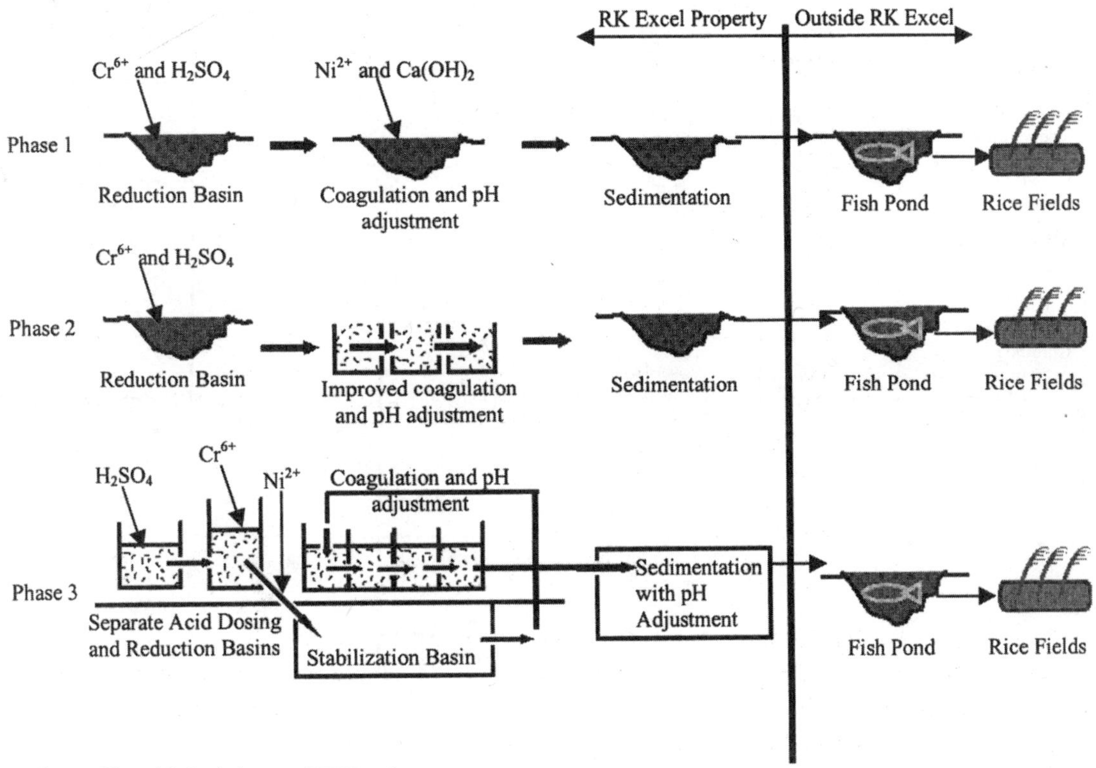

Source: Unpublished charts of RK Excel.

Phase 2: 1959 to 1969

In the late 1950s concern grew in the local community about the effects of RK Excel's effluent on receiving waters and rice fields. Farmers began to notice a decrease in rice production in fields using water drawn from a pond that received significant inflows of RK Excel's effluent. In addition, there were suspicions that the effluent was damaging fish in the pond. The farmers believed the problem was caused by wide variations in the pH of the effluent. In response to these complaints, RK Excel introduced a more reliable lime-dosing and pH neutralization system in 1959 (see Figure 4.1). In addition, it agreed to pay damages to the rice farmers affected as well as to the owner of the pond for damages to the fish. The first payment occurred in 1959, and payments continued until 1974.

The main motivation for RK Excel to make the process improvements and damage payments was to maintain good relations with the neighboring community. Most companies in Japan are quite sensitive to complaints from people living nearby. One reason is that, in Japan, changing the location of the factory is usually not a viable option; therefore, in order to carry out business in a positive atmosphere, companies must make sure that local communities are not angry with them. Many of the workers at RK Excel live close to the factory. In Japan maintaining one's social status in the local community is of utmost importance. Additionally, people are associated strongly with the companies they work for. Therefore, if RK Excel caused a problem and did not take appropriate action to resolve it, many of its workers would have been ostracized by people living nearby who were not employed by the company. There is even a word in Japanese (*murahachibu*) that describes people put into "exile" in their own communities for unacceptable actions. For

Figure 4.2 *Phase 4 of Pollution Control at RK Excel (1973 to present)*

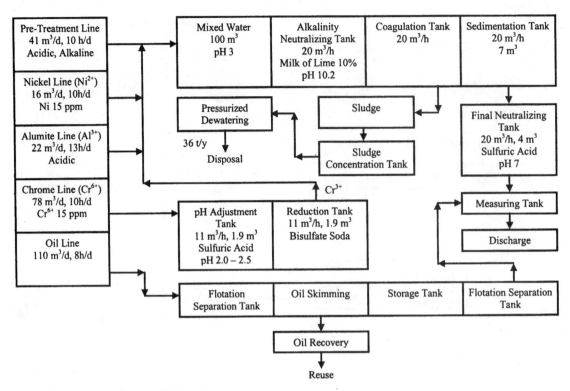

Source: Unpublished charts of RK Excel.

these reasons RK Excel was motivated to improve its environmental performance even though statutory limits were not yet in place.

Phase 3: 1970 to 1972

Japan went through a revolution in environmental consciousness in the 1960s. This was part of a worldwide trend and was also a reaction to the severe pollution problems that Japan experienced after the war. In 1970, under the new leadership of a "pro-environment" company president, Tetsuo Tanaka, RK Excel initiated a major upgrade of its pollution control processes.

The existing facilities were no longer considered "best practice" because they failed to guarantee a safe effluent quality. Markets for pollution control equipment were rapidly developing, giving the company more options than it had before. Therefore, open pits were abandoned and replaced with constructed tanks that had improved pumps and meters (see Figure 4.1). A stabilization basin was introduced to ensure an even quality of effluent to the coagulation-sedimentation tank. Additional pH neutralization was employed at the final effluent stage by introduction of sulfuric acid (H_2SO_4) dosing with a pH meter.

It is difficult to reconstruct the motivations that led RK Excel to make these changes. At first glance, it seems that national legislation, the Water Pollution Control Law of 1970, was the main motivating factor. This was the first law to include provisions for fining and shutting down noncompliant industries. Even if RK Excel could have complied with the standards (see Table 4.1) using the Phase 2 processes, it might have exceeded the standards on any given day because of the antiquated methods (earthen pits) being used. If this happened on a day of inspection, then there would have been serious consequences for RK Excel. Therefore, the changes carried out in

Phase 3 can be seen as countermeasures to reduce the risk of variability in effluent quality, and the consequent risk of noncompliance and penalties.

RK Excel, however, offers another explanation for the process upgrade in Phase 3. It notes the heightened public awareness of pollution and its dangers. The use of earthen pits came to be seen as antiquated by both the metal-plating industry and by society in general. The state of the art in pollution control had changed, and RK Excel simply wanted to keep up with industry practice and social expectations at that time. One could argue that heightened environmental consciousness led to the process changes at RK Excel and also to the Water Pollution Control Law of 1970.

Another factor that could have induced changes at RK Excel was the selection of President Tanaka as the first chairman of the Pollution Control Board of the Kusatsu Chamber of Commerce. Whether President Tanaka was selected because of his interest in pollution control or whether his interest increased because of his selection is not clear. His chairmanship, however, kept him abreast of current thinking on the environment. From his position on the Board, he would have realized the inevitable changes that were taking place at the national, prefectural, and local levels.

Phase 4: 1973 to the Present

Implementation of a fully automated pollution control system, essentially the one in place today, began in 1973. The process changes depicted in Figure 4.2 reduced variations in, and improved, effluent quality. It is possible that the Phase 4 changes were implemented to ensure compliance with the 1972 Pollution Control Ordinance of Shiga. However, RK Excel argues that in the early 1970s, automation was being introduced in most factories in Japan. It may have automated its system to save money in the long term by using less labor for pollution control and to bring RK Excel in line with the general industry practice. It is unclear what role the prefectural standards of 1972, or anticipation of the city standards of 1978, played in RK Excel's decision to automate its pollution control system.

Wastewater Quality and Effluent Standards

Table 4.1 lists the pollutants that RK Excel is regulated for as well as its pre- and post-treatment water quality. There are currently four sets of standards that RK Excel must meet: national standards based on the Water Pollution Control Law of 1970, prefectural standards based on Shiga's Pollution Control Ordinance of 1972, municipal standards based on Kusatsu's Environmental Protection Ordinance of 1978, and neighborhood standards based on the pollution control agreement (PCA) signed by RK Excel and the Yagura Town Association in 1976.

As mentioned before, the main pollutants of concern are Cr^{6+}, metals, and pH. Even without control, RK Excel's pre-treated water would meet all standards for SS, Oil, Fe^{3+}, and CN. For COD and Cu^{2+}, the national standard would be met without treatment, but the other levels are binding. All levels of standards are binding for total chromium (T-Cr), Cr^{6+}, and pH. There are no national or prefectural standards on Ni^{2+}, but the municipal and neighborhood standards are binding. The strictest standards are set by the neighborhood PCA, and RK Excel's effluent meets all of them except for Fe^{2+}, which is slightly above the required level.

From Table 4.1, it appears that RK Excel's effluent quality is constrained by the neighborhood PCA. Therefore, one could argue that if the neighborhood level of regulation did not exist, the effluent quality would be worse. The same logic can be applied to other levels such that if each successive level were removed, the effluent quality would become worse. However, as we have seen earlier, the system to attain the current quality was already in place before the PCA or before the municipal ordinance existed. Therefore, it would be incorrect to look for explanations of effluent control solely in the regulations. Indeed, the company itself claims that its pollution control efforts have been undertaken to maintain the best practices at the time.

To achieve the effluent quality shown in Table 4.1, RK Excel initially spent approximately 300 million yen on construction costs. The cost for operation and maintenance is approximately 20 million yen per year. The company's annual production cost is around 460 million yen. Therefore, operation and maintenance of pollution control equipment alone is around 4.3 percent of annual production costs. These costs do not include the costs for the groundwater remediation actions described below.

Groundwater Contamination and Remediation by RK Excel

This section describes the contamination of groundwater by hexavalent chromium caused by RK Excel and the measures taken by the company to improve water quality (see Appendix 4.1). The pollution was discovered in 1976 when residents using groundwater from household wells within 1 kilometer of the factory site complained of itchy skin and yellow well water. In response, the Shiga Prefectural Government carried out investigations and established that the groundwater in three household wells within the complaint area was contaminated. A leak of hexavalent chromium from the concrete floor of a chrome-plating tank in the factory was discovered.

An out-of-court settlement between the residents and RK Excel was reached, and compensation was paid to the affected residents. The Shiga Prefectural Government required the factory to construct new plating facilities, to treat all contaminated soil within its compound, and to pump and treat the contaminated groundwater until the concentration of hexavalent chromium met the drinking water standard. To date, the factory continues to undertake the pump-and-treat operation, and it is expected that it will take a few more years before the drinking water standard is met. The restoration of the contaminated groundwater is a costly undertaking for the factory.

Chromium Toxicity

Chromium is a heavy metal that is used in leather tanning, pigments and textile dyeing, and metal plating, for example. Chromium is used in metal plating because of its resistance to corrosion and abrasion and its pleasing appearance as well as durability. Chromium is released into the environment in its two most common oxidation states—namely, the hexavalent and trivalent forms. Both forms of chromium are very toxic and carcinogenic, with the hexavalent form being the most hazardous. Symptoms of acute dermal exposure to chromium include irritated skin and mucous membranes. Chronic exposure by inhalation can produce deep perforating nasal ulcers (known as chrome holes), bronchitis, decreased pulmonary function, pneumonia, and other respiratory problems. Ingestion can cause death. The drinking water standard for chromium in Japan is 0.05 milligrams per liter (mg/l).

Discovery of Contamination and Initial Response

During the early 1970s, the mass media in Japan widely reported contamination of soil and groundwater with heavy metals, especially at abandoned factory yards (Matsui 1993). These cases and pollution cases publicized earlier (for example, illness from Minamata and Itai Itai diseases) alarmed the Japanese people. The general public became aware of the negative effects of pollution on human health and began protesting against pollution.

Toward the end of March 1976, some residents of Yagura town (located in Kusatsu City) who were using groundwater from wells within 1 kilometer of the Shiga factory of RK Excel (then Takasago Manufacturing Co., Ltd.) began to speak out. As noted earlier, they complained that they had been suffering from skin itchiness for a period of more than one year and that the color of their well water had turned yellow. (At that time 83 percent of the 300 households in Yagura town used well water, although 97 percent of the population of Kusatsu City used piped water.) Because of the wide publicity given to pollution instances in Japan at the time, it was suspected that the groundwater was contaminated. The residents therefore requested a private company to check the quality of their well water. The analytical results revealed a concentration of hexavalent chromium of 8.2 mg/l in the well water, which was much higher than the drinking water standard of 0.05 mg/l. The results were reported to the Pollution Control Department of the Shiga Prefectural Government on March 31, 1976. The Shiga Prefectural Government immediately dispatched investigators to analyze the groundwater in six household wells within the complaint area. Concentrations of hexavalent chromium between 1.1 and 7.5 mg/l were found in the water of three of the six wells investigated—wells YG, Y, and T (Shiga Prefectural Government 1977). This confirmed the analytical results reported earlier by the residents. At a later date, water quality tests were done for all the household wells within Yagura town. Except in the three household wells already identified as being contaminated, no hexavalent chromium was detected.

On April 1, 1976, the Shiga Prefectural Government and Kusatsu City organized emergency meetings and launched an investigation. A "hexavalent chromium task force" was set up and charged with the following responsibilities:

- Provision of water supply to affected residents (Kusatsu City in charge)
- Water quality monitoring (Kusatsu City, the Kusatsu Public Health Center, and the Shiga Prefectural Environment Center in charge)
- Health check for residents (Shiga Prefectural Government and Kusatsu City in charge)
- Investigation into the cause and extent of pollution (Shiga Prefectural Government in charge, with assistance from Kusatsu City)
- Communication of information to the residents (Kusatsu City in charge).

Residents' Response

On April 3, 1976, soon after the groundwater pollution was detected, the residents of Yagura town set up a Pollution Prevention Committee to represent their interests in the investigation and mitigation of the pollution. The Pollution Prevention Committee was responsible for negotiations between the residents and RK Excel after the latter was officially identified as the source of pollution. An out-of-court settlement was reached between the residents and RK Excel; the residents acknowledged that the pollution was accidental and expressed their willingness to cooperate with RK Excel in its efforts to mitigate the problem. (RK Excel was required to perform continuous monitoring, and several residents were involved in collecting water samples from wells for analysis at the factory.)

Investigations into the Source of Pollution

The Shiga factory of RK Excel was suspected of being the polluter because it was known to be using hexavalent chromium, and it was located at a high elevation and within 1 kilometer from the polluted household wells. The Shiga Prefectural Government's investigation confirmed a leakage of hexavalent chromium from the concrete floor of a chrome-plating tank in the Shiga factory. Chromium was also detected in the soil below the tank. The factory was immediately instructed by the Shiga Prefectural Government to terminate its chrome- and nickel-plating operations and to replace the chrome-plating tanks. The company was also instructed to treat all the polluted soil within its compound.

The Shiga Prefectural Government investigated sixteen other factories in the area that were using hexavalent chromium. One of them was found to have a minor leakage of hexavalent chromium, but no contamination of the soil beneath the tank was detected. Therefore, further investigations on the source of the groundwater pollution centered on the RK Excel factory.

On April 12, 1976, the Shiga Prefectural Government started boring investigations at six locations near the RK Excel Shiga factory (wells B1 to B6), and at the three polluted household wells (wells YG, Y, and T), in order to establish the relationship between the observed leakage of hexavalent chromium at the factory and the pollution at the three household wells (see Figure 4.3). At the same time, electric probe investigations were undertaken at several locations. Based on the results of the boring and electric probe tests (also shown in Figure 4.3). RK Excel was officially identified as the source of groundwater contamination on May 28, 1976.

To determine the extent of the area of polluted groundwater, the Shiga Prefectural Government and RK Excel conducted additional electric probe investigations and boring tests (wells B7 to B13 and T1 to T6 in Figure 4.3). On September 24, 1976, the extent of the pollution was established as covering an area of 115,000 square meters.

Countermeasures by RK Excel

After the leak in the plating tank at the Shiga factory was confirmed, RK Excel, on April 5, 1976, set up a committee to investigate the accident. At the same time, the company obeyed the Shiga Prefectural Government's order to close down its nickel- and chromium-plating operations. In order to establish the extent of soil and groundwater contamination within the factory site, the company carried out boring investigations within the factory and in the neighborhood of the factory (wells T1 to T6 in Figure 4.3). As it was required to do by the Shiga Prefectural Government, the company got rid of all of the contaminated soil.

RK Excel also was required to pump-and-treat the contaminated groundwater from six wells: the three polluted household wells (YG, Y, and T) and three boring investigation wells (B7, T1, and T6) shown in Figure 4.3. These six wells had the highest concentrations of hexavalent chromium. The groundwater pumped from them was transported to the factory by trucks and then treated at the factory. RK Excel also had to monitor the quality of groundwater at five "observation wells" (B8 to B12). The treatment and monitoring of groundwater are to continue until the concentration of hexavalent chromium in the groundwater meets the drinking water quality standard of 0.05 mg/l. To meet the treatment requirement for polluted groundwater, the company expanded the capacity of its wastewater treatment facilities.

Within three months from the discovery of the hexavalent chromium pollution, RK Excel relocated its plating operations to a newly constructed facility adjacent to the old factory. It could relocate so quickly because at the time the accident was discovered, the company had already begun construction of the new facility.

Efforts to Protect Drinking Water. After the contamination of three household wells with hexavalent chromium was confirmed, Kusatsu City immediately set up temporary water supply stations for the residents of Yagura town. In addition, the Kusatsu City Public Health Center and the Shiga Prefectural Environment Center tested the water quality of 126 household wells in the area. No hexavalent chromium was detected in the water from the tested wells, but it was found that more than 30 percent of the wells did not meet the other twelve general standards for drinking water quality. (These problems were not caused by RK Excel.) Kusatsu City encouraged the residents in the area to switch from using groundwater to piped water. RK Excel met the cost of switching to piped water for the three households whose well water was contaminated.

Figure 4.3 *Location of Boring Investigation Wells and Extent of Polluted Area*

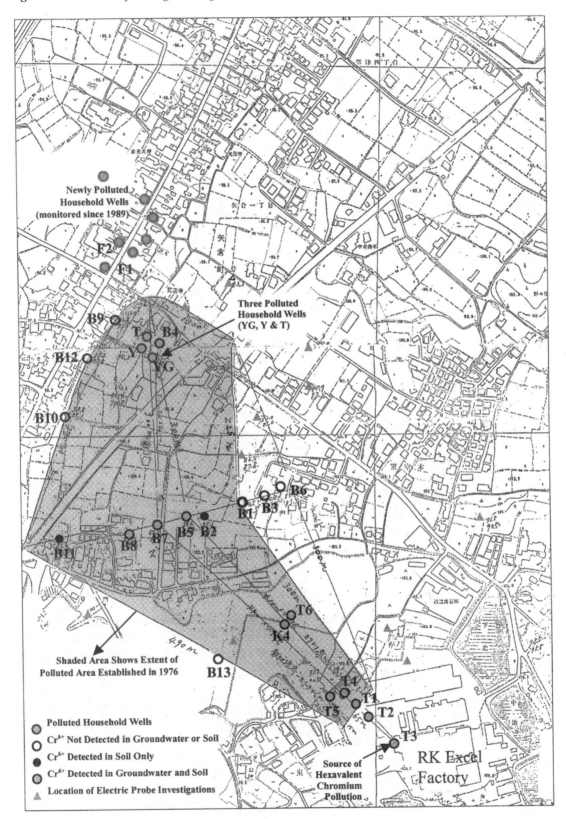

Source: Unpublished charts of Shiga Prefectural Government (1977, 1978).

MEDICAL EXAMINATION. Immediately after the groundwater in Yagura town was confirmed to be contaminated with hexavalent chromium, the Shiga Prefectural Government and Kusatsu City instituted a medical examination and health survey of the residents. Six residents were certified to be suffering from allergic and chronic dermatitis (skin disease) caused by hexavalent chromium. This was the first confirmed case in Japan of hexavalent chromium pollution. RK Excel met the costs of regular medical observation and treatment of the patients.

COMPENSATION. Negotiations concerning compensation to victims took place between the Yagura Town Pollution Prevention Committee and RK Excel under the mediation of Kusatsu City. An out-of-court settlement was reached on September 16, 1976, and the company compensated the three affected households and the Yagura town community. A total of 34 million yen was paid as compensation. In addition, RK Excel paid 11.7 million yen for the provision of piped water to the three households with contaminated well water.

Pollution Control Agreement

On November 22, 1976, a voluntary pollution control agreement was reached between the Yagura residents and RK Excel (see text of the agreement in Appendix 4.2). In this voluntary agreement RK Excel agreed to protect residents' health and the living environment by preventing pollution from its activities. Having acknowledged its social obligation to prevent pollution, the company promised to abide by all national and local laws and regulations concerning pollution control.

The PCA requires RK Excel to regularly check the quality of its effluent and make the results available to Yagura residents upon request. Representatives of the residents are allowed to visit the factory and investigate its operations. To enable residents to assess easily the quality of the effluent from the factory, the factory is required to maintain a fish-rearing pond using the effluent.

If an accident appears likely or takes place, RK Excel must undertake emergency measures and report the situation to the residents. If pollution occurs as a result of the company's activities, the company is required to take responsibility and compensate affected persons. In such a situation, the residents shall accept a fair settlement.

In addition, RK Excel is required to monitor the quality of groundwater within the polluted area and to pump-and-treat the contaminated groundwater until the concentration of hexavalent chromium meets the standard of less than 0.05 mg/l for drinking water. This operation is continuing to date.

The Battle for Recovery

TREATMENT OF CONTAMINATED SOIL AND GROUNDWATER. Polluted soil within the factory covered 240 square meters. The pollution was between 5 and 5.4 meters deep. This soil was treated by the company and discharged into the sea, a legal practice at that time. The total quantity of soil treated was 2,068 tons. RK Excel also treated the concrete floor below the leaking chromium-plating tank.

Figure 4.4 shows the quantity of water pumped from the three polluted household wells (YG, Y, and T) and the three bored wells (B7, T1, and T6). For each of these six wells, the time period of the pumping operation and the concentration of hexavalent chromium are shown in Table 4.2. The pump-and-treat operation continues at four wells (YG, Y, T, and B7), but it has been discontinued at the other two wells after the concentration of hexavalent chromium in the well water reached nondetectable levels.

Figure 4.5 shows a gradual decrease in the hexavalent chromium concentration in recent years. Figure 4.6 indicates the quality of water pumped from monitoring and observation wells.

Figure 4.4 *Quantity of Water Pumped from Pumping Wells*

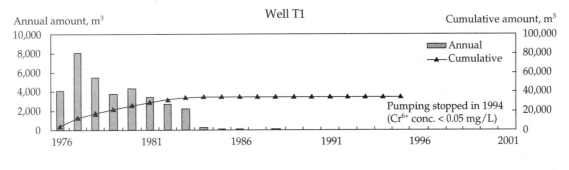

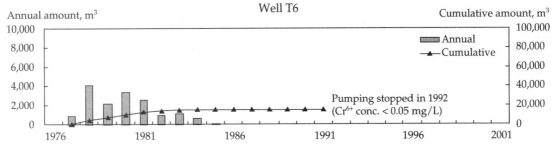

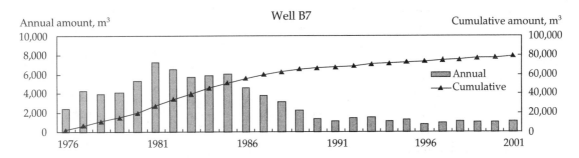

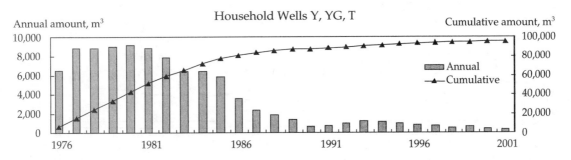

Source: Unpublished data of RK Excel.

Monitoring at wells B8 to B12 and observation at wells T2 and K4 have been going on since 1976. Hexavalent chromium concentrations in wells T2 and K4 reached levels below the drinking water standard of 0.05 mg/l in 1996. Except for well B8 (which adjoins the initially polluted well B7), no hexavalent chromium has been detected in the other monitoring wells (B9 to B12).

In 1989 observation of water quality began at several other household wells downstream of the three polluted household wells and outside the extent of the polluted area established in 1976. (The position of the wells is shown in Figure 4.3.) Data on the quality of water from two of

Figure 4.5 Quality of Water Pumped from Pumping Wells

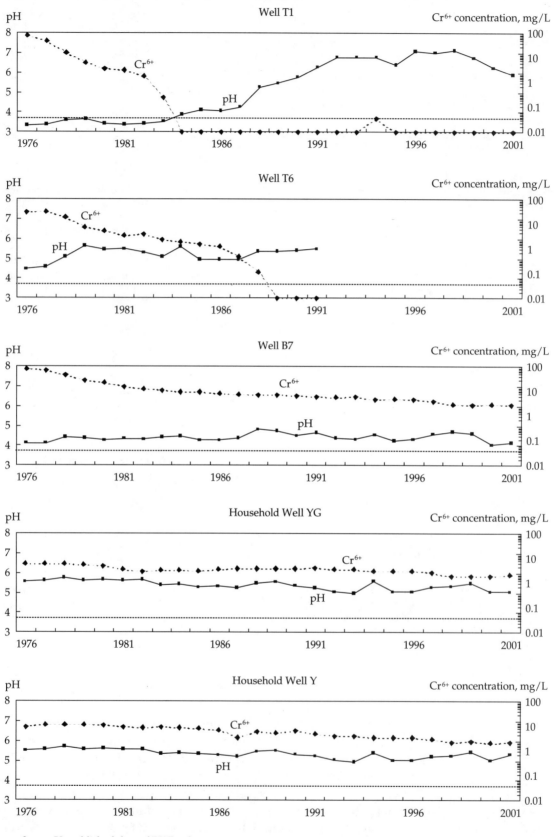

Source: Unpublished data of RK Excel.

Figure 4.6 *Quality of Water Pumped from Monitoring and Observation Wells*

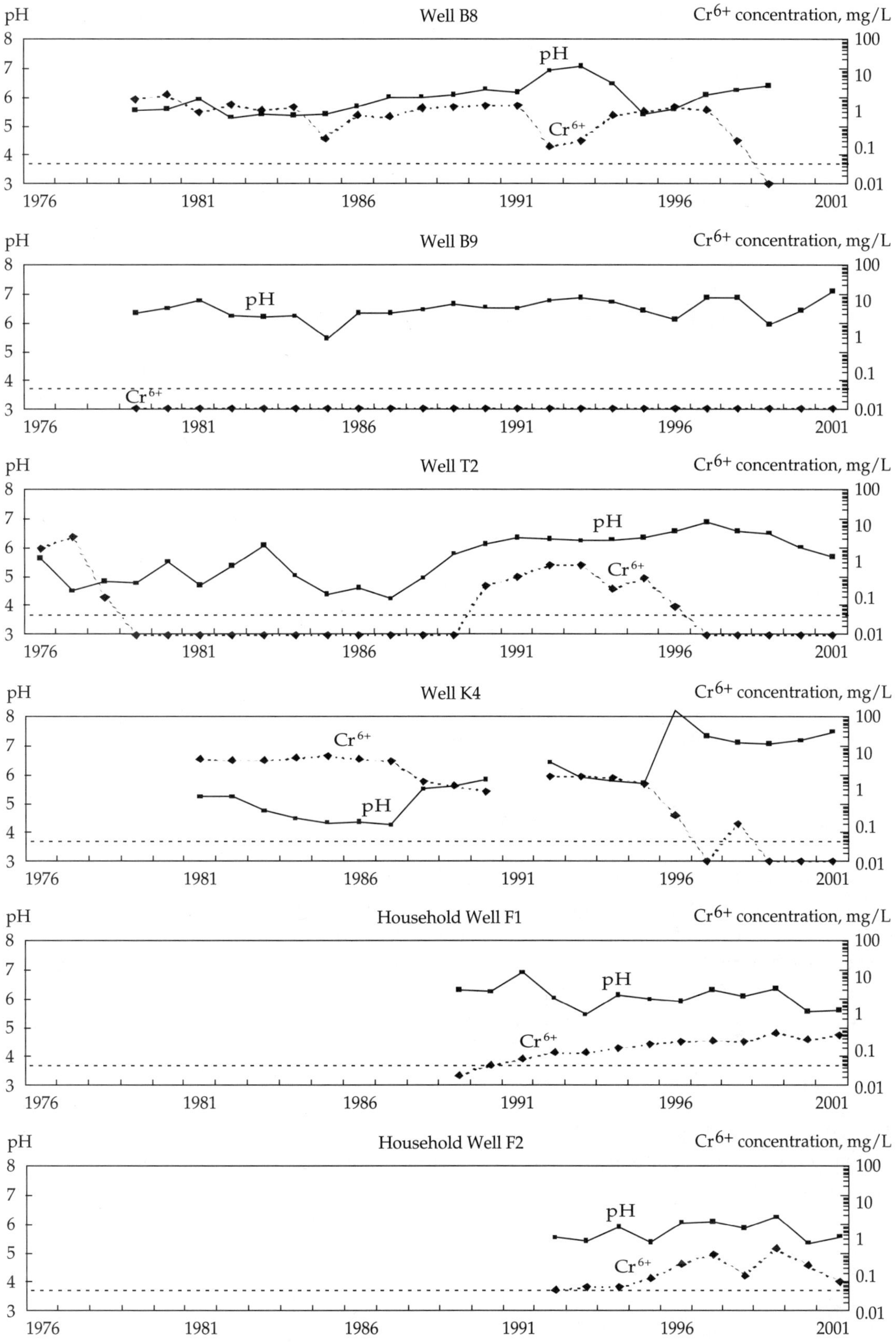

Source: Unpublished data of RK Excel.

Table 4.2 *Condition of Wells Where Polluted Groundwater Was Pumped*

		3 Polluted household wells			B7	T6	T1
		YG	Y	T	B7	T6	T1
Pumping	Start		April 6, 1976		June 5, 1976	April 25, 1976	June 12, 1976
	End	Continues to date	Continues to date	Continues to date	Continues to date	1992	1994
Water quality (Cr^{6+} conc.)	At Start of pumping	3.84 mg/l	4.02 mg/l	1.09 mg/l	54 mg/l	17.65 mg/l	74.65 mg/l
	Progress	January 1997	October 1997	April 1997	October 1997	May 1983	1984
		< 1 mg/l	< 1 mg/l	< 1 mg/l	< 1 mg/l	ND	ND
	December 1999	0.625 mg/l	0.84mg/l	0.78mg/l	0.96mg/l	Abandoned	ND
	December 2001	0.40 mg/l	0.40 mg/l	0.40 mg/l	0.50 mg/l	Abandoned	ND

ND Not detectable.
Source: Unpublished data from RK Excel.

these wells (F1 and F2) are shown in Figure 4.6, which indicates a general increase in the concentration of hexavalent chromium to levels above the drinking water standard of 0.05 mg/l. (The concentration in all these wells when the accident was discovered was below the drinking water standard.) This implies that there has been an expansion in the extent of the polluted area downstream and/or a change in the pollution pathway.

Groundwater quality is not expected to meet the drinking water quality standard for a few more years. Until this standard is met, RK Excel has an obligation to continue treating the contaminated groundwater, particularly because a few households in the area still use groundwater.

COST OF REMEDIATION. It is estimated that the company has spent between 300 million and 400 million yen in the treatment and monitoring of the groundwater since 1976. This amount is comparable to the 300 million yen incurred by the company in the construction of its current pollution control system. These costs, and the cost of treating the contaminated soil and compensating residents, has been borne solely by the company. This is an expensive undertaking for the company, particularly during the current economic recession in Japan.

Conclusion

This chapter, like Chapter 3, has focused on the importance of social pressure in influencing dischargers to control pollution. Although the environmental laws and regulations of Japan have had an unmistakably positive effect on effluent quality, strong social pressure and the fear of being ostracized by the community have motivated polluting industries to address the problems they have caused.

This case study of groundwater pollution caused by RK Excel suggests a valuable lesson: *pollution prevention* is easier and less expensive than *pollution remediation*. It also is clear that adverse pollution impacts do not necessarily have to be mitigated in the most cost-effective way. Some residents are still using groundwater and are not willing to change to piped water even though they would be adequately compensated for making the switch. RK Excel is required to continue treating the contaminated groundwater until the concentration of hexavalent chromium meets the drinking water standard, irrespective of whether the groundwater is used for domestic purposes or not.

Certainly, it may be argued that remedial measures for pollution should be evaluated based on a cost-benefit analysis. But in this case and in many pollution cases in Japan, remedial actions have been taken in response to social and/or political pressure, or as a response to accidents. Less consideration has been given to the monetary costs involved. Like Japan in the 1970s, many developing countries today are beginning to face the challenge of harmonizing development and environmental conservation. The Japanese pollution control experience holds a valuable lesson for these countries—namely, that in the long term it costs more to clean up pollution than to prevent it.

Appendix 4.1
Chronology of Events Related to Contamination
of Groundwater by RK Excel, 1976

Initial Actions

End of March	Some residents of Yagura town complained of itchy skin and yellow well water. They hired a private company to analyze the water. The results revealed a hexavalent chromium concentration of 8.2 mg/l. (The drinking water standard is 0.05 mg/l.)
March 31	Results of the water quality analysis were reported to the Pollution Control Department of the Shiga Prefectural Government. Kusatsu City and the Shiga Prefecture collected groundwater samples from six household wells. Water in three of them was found to be contaminated with hexavalent chromium at concentrations of between 1.1 and 7.5 mg/l.
April 1	The Shiga Prefectural Government and Kusatsu City organized emergency meetings and launched an investigation. A "hexavalent chromium task force" was set up and charged with the following responsibilities: provision of water supply, monitoring of water quality, health check for residents, investigation into the cause and extent of pollution, and communication of information to residents.
April 3	Residents set up a Pollution Prevention Committee.

Water Supply Actions

April 1	Kusatsu City set up water supply stations for residents.
April 1–4	Groundwater analysis for 126 household wells within Yagura town was carried out. Hexavalent chromium was detected in only three household wells.
April 6-9	Tap water was provided to the three affected households.

Investigation into Pollution Source

April 1–4	Investigations were conducted at the Shiga factory of RK Excel. A leak was found under the area where chrome plating was being carried out. The factory was ordered to stop its plating operations.
April 12	Boring investigations and electric probe investigations began.
May 28	RK Excel was officially identified as the source of groundwater contamination based on the results of the boring and electric probe tests.
Sept. 24	The extent of the polluted area was established as 115,000 square meters.

RK Excel's Response

April 5	The factory established a committee to investigate the accident.
April 6	Treatment of contaminated soil within the factory began; the factory disposed of all contaminated soil.
	Treatment of groundwater from the three contaminated household wells began. (Hexavalent chromium concentrations were 8.08, 5.46, and 0.36 mg/l at the start of the treatment.) The water was pumped and then transported by trucks for treatment at the factory. The treated water was returned to the wells. (This treatment continues to date.)
June 6	In a letter to the mayor of Kusatsu City, the factory admitted responsibility and apologized for the pollution of soil in some of the investigated sites.
End of June	RK Excel began nickel- and chromium-plating operations at a newly built facility.
Nov. 18	The factory submitted its wastewater treatment plan to the Shiga Prefectural Government.
Nov. 8	Treatment of contaminated soil within the former factory site was completed.

Medical Examination

April 2	Medical examination of the residents of Yagura town was performed. (Thirteen persons were examined.)
April 8	Health survey for the residents was done. (Fifteen additional people were surveyed.)
April 28	First close medical examination of victims (that is, of the residents with the contaminated wells) was performed. (Four persons were examined.)
May 14	Four persons were certified as having allergic and chronic dermatitis (skin disease). For the residents who had been exposed to hexavalent chromium for more than one year, a cause-effect relationship was established between the pollution and their illness.
June–July	Second close medical examination was carried out. (Nine persons were examined.)
August 28	Two more persons were certified as having allergic and chronic dermatitis.

Compensation

July 27	Yagura Town Pollution Prevention Committee asked Takasago (the former name of RK Excel) for compensation and provision of piped water to affected households. Takasago paid 11.7 million yen for provision of piped water supply to the three affected households.
Sept. 6	An out-of-court settlement was reached. RK Excel paid 34 million yen to the affected families.

Voluntary Pollution Control Agreement

Nov. 22	Yagura town community and RK Excel signed a voluntary pollution control agreement (see Appendix 4.2).

Appendix 4.2
Pollution Control Agreement

The Yagura Neighborhood Association of Kusatsu City and RK Excel, Co., Ltd. (formerly known as Takasago, Inc.), in order to control pollution caused by the latter, collaborated on the following pollution control agreement.

(Purpose)

Article 1. In order to preserve the health of local inhabitants as well as the natural environment, the purpose of this agreement shall be to control the occurrence of pollution generated by the activities of RK Excel.

(Background)

Article 2. RK Excel, recognizing its social responsibility for the pollution resulting from its activities, shall make the best efforts to control the pollution.

Paragraph 2. Based on the previous paragraph, RK Excel shall obey the various pollution control laws and ordinances as well as the administrative guidance of Shiga Prefecture and Kusatsu City and it shall positively cooperate with the request of the Yagura Neighborhood Association.

Paragraph 3. The Yagura Neighborhood Association shall positively cooperate with RK Excel on Paragraph 1, Article 2.

(Implementation of pollution control measures)

Article 3. RK Excel shall observe the standards (mentioned at the end of this document) given in Chapter 2 of the Pollution Control Agreement on Paragraph 2, Article 1. Also, RK Excel shall examine and control its facilities with meticulous care.

(Monitoring and reporting)

Article 4. RK Excel shall monitor the air and water discharged from its facilities and report the result to the Yagura Neighborhood Association upon request.

(Spot inspections)

Article 5. RK Excel, notified beforehand, shall allow and cooperate with spot inspections within necessary limits carried out by a designated Pollution Inspector chosen by the Yagura Neighborhood Association.

Paragraph 2. The supervisors shall comply with guidance provided by RK Excel staff for security reasons during inspection.

(Measures to be undertaken during an accident)

Article 6. In the event of equipment breakdown or occurrence of an accident, RK Excel shall take emergency measures and immediately make efforts to restore proper operation. Any incident shall be immediately reported to the Yagura Neighborhood Association.

(Trouble-shooting and compensation)

Article 7. When the residents in the area complain of pollution due to RK Excel or RK Excel damages the residents, RK Excel shall immediately take appropriate countermeasures and settle the problem with sincerity. Also RK Excel shall compensate damages and the Yagura Neighborhood Association shall cooperate to reach a settlement.

(Obligation for the inspection of monitoring wells and groundwater)

Article 8. As the groundwater of the Yagura area has been polluted with Chromium (VI), RK Excel shall carry out sampling of Chromium (VI) concentrations at five monitoring wells (No. 8, 9, 10, 11, and 12) and of groundwater for groundwater users until the concentration of Chromium (VI) meets the drinking water quality standard of 0.05 mg/l.

(Establishment of monitoring pool)

Article 9. RK Excel shall make a pool in its factory area to pour all the discharge within three years and stock the pool with fish so that the Yagura Neighborhood Association can easily judge whether the discharge from RK Excel is harmless or not.

(Information Disclosure)

Article 10. RK Excel shall disclose the condition of its pollution control measures when requested by the Yagura Neighborhood Association.

(Others)

Article 11. When the matters which are not determined in this agreement or any doubt about the interpretation of this agreement arise, the Yagura Neighborhood Association and RK Excel shall confer and decide.

To certify this agreement, both Parties shall sign in duplicate and retain one copy.

(Table of Standards)

Air pollution control

K value	Less than 5
Soot	Less than $0.2g/Nm^3$
Sulfur contained in fuel	Less than 1.8%
Chromium and Nickel in soot	Not detected

Water pollution control

pH	6.0 – 8.0
BOD	Less than 30 ppm
COD	Less than 30 ppm
SS	Less than 30 ppm
Oil (Mineral Oil)	Less than 3ppm
Chromium (VI)	Less than 0.05ppm
Nickel	Less than 1ppm
Cu and Zn	Less than 0.1ppm

Offensive odor control

Odor Intensity*	Less than 2.5

*Levels of Odor Intensity between 2.5 and 3.5, according to Japan's Ministry of the Environment, are levels at which the majority of residents do not feel uncomfortable. See Environment Ministry (www.env.go.sp/en/lar/regulation/odor.html#2-2).

Authorized and signed by:
  Seiichi Yoshikawa
  Chairman
  The Yagura Neighborhood Association
  Tetsuo Tanaka
  Representative Director
  RK Excel
  Higashida
  Witness
  Chief
  Kusatsu City Transport and Pollution Control Division

(Memorandum of Understanding)

Based on the Article 8 in Pollution Control Agreement, the Yagura Neighborhood Association and RK Excel agree as follows:

RK Excel shall bear the cost for inspection of monitoring wells and groundwater. The Yagura Neighborhood Association shall be present at inspections and cooperate.

RK Excel shall pay 1,500 yen per person for one time to witnesses above mentioned as cooperation fee. The fee will be calculated every six months and paid before the end of the seventh month.

When both parties recognize that the amount of the cooperation fee above mentioned has become markedly unsuitable because of fluctuation or unexpected cause, both parties shall discuss an amendment.

To certify this MOU, both parties shall sign in duplicate and retain one copy.

November 22, 1976

Note

1. Most of the information in the chapter comes from unpublished data provided by RK Excel Co., Ltd.

References

Matsui, S. 1993. "Pollution Control in Japan: A Historical Perspective." In *Environmental Pollution Control: The Japanese Experience*. Papers presented at the UNU International Symposium on Eco-Restructuring, July 5–7, 1993. Tokyo, Japan: The United Nations University.

Shiga Prefectural Government. 1977. "Groundwater Contamination by Hexavalent Chromium" (in Japanese). In *White Paper on Environment*. Otsu, Japan: Shiga Prefectural Government.

———. 1978. *Hexavalent Chromium Pollution Record (in Japanese)*. Kusatsu, Japan: Shiga Prefectural Government, Kusatsu Public Health Center.

5

Economic Incentives to Promote Compliance: Japan's Environmental Soft Loan Program

Akihisa Mori, Soo Cheol Lee, and Kazuhiro Ueta

During the 1970s, Japan swiftly reduced air pollution from sulfur dioxide—an accomplishment often cited as an example of successful environmental policy (Janicke and Weidner 1995). This success can be attributed in part to Japan's environmental soft loan program. In this chapter we address two questions. First, how influential is the incentive effect in firms' decisions to invest in pollution control equipment? Second, what are the preconditions for an environmental soft loan programs? By focusing on these questions, we hope to shed light on the contribution of soft loans in the total system of environmental policies in Japan.

Soft Loans by Public Financial Institutions for Pollution Abate ment Investments

Through national systems and credit trusts (such as postal savings and national pension funds), Japan's central government has collected savings at low cost and allocated them to public financial institutions such as the Japan Development Bank (JDB) and the Japan Financial Corporation for Small Business (JFCSB). Then these institutions lend out the money to industries that often have had difficulties obtaining financing on a commercial basis. Specialized public financial institutions usually offer more favorable terms of interest than do private financial institutions. In the postwar period they helped finance strategic industries, such as electricity, steel, coal mining, and shipping. During the 1970s, when industrial pollution alarmed the Japanese people and became the focus of government policy, public financial institutions expanded the type of funds or lending facilities to include pollution abatement investment.

As shown in Table 5.1, JDB (which includes the Hokkaido and Tohoku Development Corporation) provided environmental soft loans for big businesses, while the JFCSB, the People's Finance Corporation, and the Japan Small Business Corporation provided them for small businesses. The only public financial institution specializing in environmental soft loans is the Japan Environment Corporation, formerly the Environment Pollution Control Service Corporation. Among the public financial institutions that provided environmental soft loans, JEC, JDB, and JFCSB were the most important. For example, in 1975 they accounted for 95 percent of all of the environmental soft loans that were offered.

Environmental soft loans are for capital investments only. They do not cover operation and maintenance (O&M) expenses, usually two to three times more than the cost of building pollution control facilities (Konishi 1996). Loan ratios, interest rates, and redemption periods vary by firm size, type of facilities, and type of usage (for example, joint or individual investment).

Until the 1970s, the lending rate of the public financial institutions was set in between the borrowing rate from the Fiscal Investment and Loan Program and the most preferential lending rate of private banks. The lending rate was usually 1 to 2 percentage points lower than the long-term prime interest rate for big firms, and about 2 to 3 percentage points lower than the rate for small and medium-size enterprises of SMEs (see Table 5.2). The lending rate set by JDB and

Table 5.1 Environmental Soft Loans by Specialized Public Financial Institutions

Loan agency	Loan customer (borrower)	Main facility for loan	Loan ratio[a]	Loan interest rate[b]	Redemption period[c]	Loan ceiling
Japan Environment Corporation	Big business, small business, local government	Joint pollution control facility	Big business: 70%, others: 80%	Big business: 8.2%, others: 5.0%	Machinery: 15 years, others: 20 years	None
		Individual pollution control facility	Big business: 50%, others: 80%	Big business: 8.2%, others: 6.3%	Within 15 years	None
		Industrial waste disposal facility	Same as above	4.5%–8.7 %	Within 15 years	None
Japan Development Bank	Big business	Pollution control facility	50%	8.7%	About 10 years	None
		Waste recycling facility	50%	9.9%	About 10 years	None
		Moving of polluting facility	50%	9.0%	Within 15 years	None
		Industrialization of new technology[d]	50%	8.0%	10–15 years	None
Japan Financial Corporation for Small Business	Small business	Pollution control facility	None	7.5%	Within 15 years	150 million yen
		Moving of polluting facility	None	8.4%–9.4%	Within 15 years	150 million yen
		Industrialization of new technology[d]	None	8.5%	Within 15 years	150 million yen
People's Finance Corporation	Small business	Pollution control facility	None	7.5%	Within 15 years	18 million yen
		Moving of polluting facility	None	8.4%–9.4%	Within 15 years	18 million yen
		Industrialization of new technology[d]	None	8.5%	Within 15 years	18 million yen
Japan Small Business Corporation	Small business	Joint pollution control facility	80%	No interest	Within 20 years	None
		Collective factory	65%	2.7%	Within 20 years	None
		Lease of pollution control facility	65%	2.7%	Within 12 years	None

a. The ratio of the loan to the total investment cost.
b. Loan criteria were as of the end of March 1997. Loan interest criteria were as of the end of March 1975, when the environmental soft loans were provided most actively. Currently, most lending rates from public financial institutions are about 3 percent.
c. Including a grace period of one to three years.
d. Loan to promote dissemination of new technology.
Source: Lee (1999).

Table 5.2 *Lending and Borrowing Rates of the Environmental Soft Loan Program*

(percent)

Year	Long-term preferential interest rate	Borrowing rate from Fiscal Investment and Loan Program	JDB rate	Rates of JEC's Individual Pollution Control Facility			JFCSB rate	Rates of Japan Small Business Corporation
				Big business	Small business	Local government		
1965	8.3	6.5	7.5	7.5	7.0	7.0		0–2.7
1966	8.0	6.5	7.0	7.5	7.0	7.0		0–2.7
1967	7.9	6.5	7.0	7.0	6.5	7.0		0–2.7
1968	7.9	6.5	7.0	7.0	6.5		7.0	0–2.7
1969	8.1	6.5	7.0	7.0	6.0		7.0	0–2.7
1970	8.2	6.5	7.0	7.0	6.0		7.0	0–2.7
1971	8.5	6.5	7.0	7.0	6.0		7.0	0–2.7
1972	8.5	6.5	7.0	7.0	6.0		7.0	0–2.7
1973	7.7	6.2	7.2	6.7	5.5		6.7	0–2.7
1974	9.4	7.5	8.2	7.7	6.0		7.2	0–2.7
1975	9.9	8.0	8.7	8.2	6.3		7.5	0–2.7
1976	9.2	7.5	8.2	7.7	6.0		7.2	0–2.7
1977	9.2	7.5	8.2	7.7	6.0		7.2	0–2.7
1978	7.6	6.5	7.2	6.7	5.75		7.0	0–2.7
1979	7.1	6.05	6.75	6.25	5.75		6.55	0–2.7
1980	8.8	8.0	8.7	7.35	6.5		8.3	0–2.7
1981	8.8	8.0	8.7	8.2	7.35		8.5	0–2.7
1982	8.4	7.3	8.0	7.5	6.65		7.8	0–2.7
1983	8.4	7.3	8.0	7.5	6.65		7.8	0–2.7
1984	7.9	7.1	7.8	7.3	6.45		7.6	0–2.7
1985	7.4	7.1	7.3	7.2	6.45	5.45	7.6	0–2.7
1986	6.4	6.05	6.3	6.2	5.65	5.15	6.3	0–2.7
1987	5.2	5.2	5.2	5.2	4.85	4.65	5.2	0–2.7
1988	5.5	5.0	5.4	5.2	4.6	4.5	5.4	0–2.7
1989	5.7	4.85	5.55	5.05	4.55	4.4	5.35	0–2.7
1990	7.5	6.2	6.9	6.4	5.65	5.3	6.7	0–2.7
1991	7.5	6.6	7.3	6.8	6.0	5.55	7.1	0–2.7
1992	6.0	5.5	5.9	5.8	5.15	4.75	5.9	0–2.7
1993	4.9	4.4	4.8	4.7	4.3	4.3	4.8	0–2.7
1994	4.4	4.3	4.4	4.4	4.2	4.2	4.35	0–2.7
1995	4.5	4.65	4.2	4.65	4.45	4.45	4.2	0–2.7
1996	3.2	3.4	3.4	3.4	3.4	3.4	3.4	0–2.7

Note: The rates are the standard rates at the end of March (the end of the fiscal year in Japan). The loan rate for investment in pollution control facilities was, for the first two to three years, 0.1 to 0.5 percentage point lower than the rate shown in the table. The interest rate of JEC loans to local government is for industrial waste treatment facilities. The 2.7 interest rate of JSBC is for lease business funds for pollution control facilities.

Sources: Ministry of Finance (1975–96) and public financial institutions.

JFCSB was usually higher than the borrowing rate. On the other hand, the Japan Environment Corporation (JEC) and the Japan Small Business Corporation set a lending rate lower than the borrowing rate to reduce the financial cost for SMEs.

The Subsidy Effect of the Preferential Interest Rate

As already mentioned, soft loans by public financial institutions can be made at a preferential interest rate. Usually, the floating interest rate is applied for loans from private banks in any loan period, while a fixed rate is set for loans from public financial institutions throughout the repayment period. Consequently, the effect of the preferential interest rate is the present value of the difference between the fixed preferential rates of public financial institutions (prime rate) and the floating market rates of private banks throughout the repayment period.

The difference, DP_k (the effect of preferential interest rate in k-period), can be calculated, according to Matsuno (1997), as

(1) $$DP_k = (1 - t) \cdot I \cdot e \cdot [1 - (k - 1)/m] \cdot (i - i\#),$$

where t is corporation tax rate, I is the firm's pollution abatement investment, e is the loan ratio of the soft loan, i is the open market rate, $i\#$ is the preferential interest rate of the soft loan, and m is the repayment period.

With discount rate j, the discount factor r is described as $r = 1/(1 + j)$. Thus, the total sum of present value DP for the preferential interest rate can be calculated,

(2) $$DP = (1 - t) \cdot I \cdot e \cdot (i - i\#) \cdot S(1 - (k - 1)/m) \cdot r^k$$
$$= (1 - t) \cdot I \cdot e \cdot (i - i\#) \cdot [r/(1 - r)] \cdot \{1 - r/(1 - r) \cdot [(1 - r^m)/m]\}.$$

Because estimation of the open market rate (i) from the time of the loan until the repayment period is very difficult, the effect of the preferential interest rate for soft loans is calculated with equation 1 for every period (k), from the time of the loan until the repayment period, and then added up by fiscal year.

With borrowing from public financial institutions, the taxable profit usually increases because of the reduction in interest expense, and therefore the tax liability increases. This influence, however, is not considered in our calculation (that is, $t = 0$). Concerning firms' pollution abatement investment (I) and loan ratio (e), we use the amount of soft loan ($I \cdot e$), as the total amount. As for the open market rate, we adopt the long-term prime rate of private banks. In addition, we use the standard rate as of the end of March (the end of the Japanese fiscal year) and suppose that the open market rate does not vary during the year. We also assume that soft loans are provided at the end of March and are repaid by an equal amount over ten years. All data are calculated with current value.

The subsidy effect of the preferential interest rate was JP¥ 80.6 billion during 1965–79 and JP¥ 22 billion in 1975 alone (see Table 5.3). It amounted to more than 5 percent of the environmental soft loan provided in 1975. The amount of subsidization was largest in JEC, about JP¥ 54 billion during 1965–79, followed by JDB and JFCSB. JDB provided an environmental soft loan more than twice the amount of JEC's loan. This was possible because of a lower lending rate.

Since the late 1970s, however, the effect of the preferential interest rate has become negative: that is, firms should pay more than they borrowed, which is what usually happens with loans from private financial institutions. The amount of negative subsidization was largest in JDB— JP¥ 3.8 billion throughout the period from 1965 to 1995. JEC also provided negative subsidization from 1986 to 1989 and from 1993 to 1995 (see Table 5.3).

Although this contradicts the conventional wisdom, a soft loan does not always provide a subsidy to borrowers. Many of the loans were made in the 1960s when private interest rates were

Table 5.3 *The Cumulative Effect of the Preferential Interest Rate for Soft Loans,*
by Public Financial Institution

(100 million yen)

Year	Total	Japan Environment Corporation	Japan Development Bank	Japan Financial Corporation for Small Business
1965	0.2	0.1	0.1	—
1966	0.6	0.4	0.2	—
1967	1.4	1.2	0.2	—
1968	2.4	2.0	0.4	—
1969	5.7	4.3	1.4	—
Subtotal	10.3	8.0	2.3	—
1970	11.0	9.1	1.7	0.2
1971	24.8	18.6	5.2	1.0
1972	40.6	26.1	11.1	3.4
1973	37.4	25.7	8.8	2.9
1974	139.3	75.9	48.0	15.4
1975	219.9	118.5	80.3	21.1
1976	184.7	104.4	62.3	18.0
1977	178.1	105.2	54.0	18.9
1978	4.9	35.3	−34.8	4.4
1979	−34.6	17.3	−52.5	0.6
Subtotal	806.1	536.1	184.1	85.9
1980	157.3	86.1	56.5	14.7
1981	135.0	78.1	44.6	12.3
1982	86.1	59.0	20.2	6.9
1983	79.4	55.2	17.9	6.3
1984	27.3	33.6	−7.3	1.0
1985	−19.6	10.0	−26.8	−2.8
1986	−92.7	−19.4	−64.1	−9.2
1987	−154.9	−40.6	−99.8	−14.5
1988	−92.6	−22.2	−60.9	−9.5
1989	−53.4	−5.1	−43.0	−5.3
Subtotal	71.9	234.7	−162.7	−0.1
1990	96.8	60.1	24.8	11.9
1991	104.0	59.6	32.9	11.5
1992	1.7	11.8	−7.8	−2.3
1993	−72.3	−21.1	−41.7	−9.5
1994	−88.1	−32.1	−41.1	−14.9
1995	−60.2	−20.4	−28.6	−11.2
Subtotal	−18.1	57.9	−61.5	−14.5
Total	870.2	836.7	−37.8	71.3

Source: Lee (1999).

higher. Since many firms had locked in to fixed rates, they often did not have the option to restructure or refinance when private rates fell in the later periods. After the 1990s, an increasing number of borrowing firms tried to make early repayment of their loans because of the financial cost burden caused by the negative effect of the preferential interest rate.[1]

The Impact of Soft Loans on Pollution Abatement Investment

In this section we try to evaluate quantitatively the incentive effect of soft loans on pollution abatement investments. The amount of the soft loans provided and the preferential interest rates are explanatory variables. The difference between the long-term prime rate used by private banks and the Japan Development Bank's lending rate is included in the equation as a proxy for preference. We also add the reductions in national tax revenues caused by the special taxation measures since these measures play an important role in encouraging pollution abatement investments.[2] The estimation period is 1968 to 1993, and the investment function is specified in logarithmic form so that the coefficients show the elasticity of investment with respect to each independent variable. We adjust the variables using the gross domestic product (GDP) deflator. The function for pollution abatement investment can be expressed

$$(3) \qquad Ln(X/P) = a + bLn(M/P) + gLn(T/P) + dLn(r-i),$$

where X is the total amount of investment for pollution control facilities by big business in 100 million yen (current price). This amount is based on research by the Ministry of Economy, Trade, and Industry (METI), formerly the Ministry of International Trade and Industry. In Equation 3, P is the GDP deflator (index: 1995 = 100), M is the total amount of soft loans to big business (in 100 million yen, current price), T is the estimated decrease in tax revenues brought about by the special taxation measures for pollution control facilities (in 100 million yen, current price), r is the long-term prime interest rate per year, and i is the annual lending rate for pollution control offered by JDB.

The calculated results are shown in Equation 4. The t-values for the coefficients are shown in parentheses.

$$(4) \qquad Ln(X/P) = 4.622 + 0.521Ln(M/P) + 0.057Ln(T/P) + 0.126Ln(r-i),$$
$$(5.665) \quad (3.892) \qquad\qquad (0.557) \qquad\qquad (2.238)$$

$$r = 0.7283$$
$$DW = 1.990$$
$$R^2 = 0.985$$

The amount of soft loans is significant at the 1 percent level, and the preferential interest rate is significant at the 5 percent level. The coefficients of both variables are positive, which indicates that they had a positive impact on pollution abatement investments. The influence of the special taxation measures was not significant. In addition, the coefficient of the amount of the loan (0.521) is bigger than that of the special tax reduction (0.057) and that of the preferential interest rate (0.126). The incentive effect of the soft loan, among the independent variables, proved to be the greatest. As a long-term, stable financial resource, the soft loan has enabled firms to invest in pollution abatement and thus comply with tightening environmental regulations (see Figure 5.1).

Although statistically significant, the effect of a preferential interest rate, which is said to be an economic advantage of environmental soft loans, was not as high as expected. It should be noted, however, that preferential interest rates for SMEs are not reflected in Equation 4: the effect of the preferential interest rate for them may be bigger than indicated in this estimation.

Figure 5.1 *Relation between Pollution Abatement Investment by Big Businesses and Environmental Soft Loans, 1968–93*

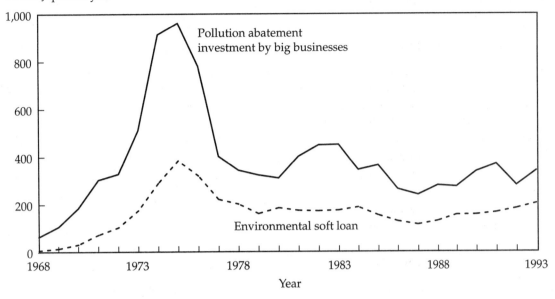

Billion Japanese yen

Source: The amount of pollution abatement investment by big business is based on research by the Ministry of Economy, Trade, and Industry (formerly the Ministry of International Trade and Industry). The amount of environmental soft loans to big businesses by public financial institutions is also based on research by METI.

Features of Japan's Environmental Soft Loan Program

Loans to Reduce Investment Costs

Environmental soft loans followed the establishment of new environmental regulations and stricter standards (see Table 5.4). For example, soft loans were provided in 1968 after the K-value regulation of sulfur dioxide[3] and in 1974 after the introduction of total emission load control. The loans enabled firms complying with the tightened regulations to reduce their investment costs. Implementing environmental regulations in close connection to affordable loans as one "package" is the first feature of Japan's environmental soft loan program.

Japanese firms faced fierce opposition from local residents who were upset about worsening pollution and the construction of factories. To maintain economic growth, the government had no choice but to set new regulations and tighten standards so that local residents would be convinced that pollution reduction could be achieved rapidly. Firms, however, were required to make huge investments in order to comply with the new regulations to control pollution. The environmental soft loan program lowered the financial costs for firms to invest in pollution abatement. The program would not have been implemented had it not matched the firms' investment needs, and the investments would not have been made rapidly if the supply of loan funds had fallen short of demand. Therefore, the Ministry of Economy, Trade, and Industry designed the environmental soft loan program based on information on demand that was supplied by specialized public financial institutions.[4]

The regulation–soft loan connection or "package" (see Table 5.4) and the government-business information sharing system facilitated a quick response by companies to regulations. Pollution

Table 5.4 *The Regulation-Loan Connection*

Year	Regulation	Associated environmental soft loan	Public financial institution
1958	Regulations for water pollution control enacted		
1960		Loan offered for sewage treatment facility	JDB
1962	Smoke Control Law enacted		
1963		Loan offered for smoke control facility	JDB
1965		Environmental low-interest loans offered	JEC
1968	Air Pollution Control Law enacted K-value regulation for SO_x Noise Regulation Law enacted	Loan offered for the fuel conversion to crude oil with low-sulfur content and for the construction of a desulfurization plant	JDB
1970	Water Pollution Control Law enacted; Waste Disposal and Public Cleansing Law enacted	Loan offered for flue gas desulfurization	JDB
1971	Regulations for toxic metal, BOD, COD, SS	Setting a credit line for pollution control loan, as a targeted loan item	JDB
1974	Introduction of total emission load control for SO_x	Loan offered for industrial waste disposal	JEC
1981	Introduction of total emission load control for NO_x		
1983	Septic tank regulation enacted	Loan offered for energy saving	JFCSB
1988		Joint treatment septic tank (for groups of factories) added as loan target	JEC
1991	Law for energy saving and recycling enacted	Loan offered for joint service of industrial waste treatment facility and founding of green district	JEC

Source: Lee (1999).

rapidly declined. It is noteworthy that the soft loan program began in response to the rapid industrialization of the 1960s and its devastating effect upon the environment. Since then loans have been offered whenever the government has directed its focus to pollution abatement.

Loans for Investment in "Standardized" Technology

Environmental soft loans are provided to firms to invest in a designated "pollution abatement" technology; a firm's pollution reduction performance is not considered. This is the second feature of Japan's environmental soft loan program.

Lending decisions proceed as follows. METI evaluates the performance of a particular technology. (Earlier METI had either contracted out to develop this pollution abatement technology, or the technology had been developed directly by private firms.) If the technology is found to reduce pollution significantly, METI then designates the technology as "standardized." Public financial institutions provide soft loans to firms applying for loans to finance investments in standardized technology.

ADVANTAGES. A soft loan program for standardized technology has numerous advantages. It enables firms to comply with regulations. It also enables the government to disseminate to firms, especially small and medium-size enterprises, information on pollution abatement technologies and their performance. If they have sound information in advance, firms can avoid losses from investing in technologies that are cost ineffective or underdeveloped.

A soft loan program also promotes the development of a pollution abatement technology industry. Demand for the abatement technology inevitably grows once it is designated as a standard, and a soft loan is available for investing in it. This will enable the industry to expand production and become competitive, enhancing its technological and financial standing.

Another advantage of the soft loan program is that it eases the loan appraisal process for public financial institutions with limited capacity to appraise environmental technology. JDB and JFCSB do not employ personnel with special expertise for appraising the technological aspects of investment. JEC, on the other hand, employs people with expertise to appraise the technology. JDB and JFCSB appraise the technology only in reference to a list of technical standards.[5] These two institutions participate in the environmental soft loan program because they benefit from the detailed environmental technology assessments made by other institutions in the program, such as JEC.

DISADVANTAGES. The soft loan program for the standardized technology also has some disadvantages. End-of-pipe technology tends to be designated as a technical standard because firms can employ it relatively easily. Indeed, firms tend not to invest in production process adjustments and in a clean production technology right at the outset, although this technology may actually entail a lower abatement cost than that of a standardized technology. As a result, most firms have undertaken pollution abatement investments twice: first, they invest in the standardized technology to obtain the soft loan and to comply with the environmental regulations; second, they invest in the production change to reduce the operation and maintenance cost for pollution abatement (Mori 2002).

Such duplication of investments should be considered in the context of the times. Firms were strongly obliged to control pollution. Japan's serious pollution had ruined the environment as well as many people's health, and the public outcry against these wrongs was strong. Fierce legal battles were waged against polluters. In light of the severity of the pollution levels, firms and the government had limited time to conduct research or to develop cost-effective pollution abatement technologies. Production process changes and clean production technology required an even longer research period than end-of-pipe technology because of their firm-specific nature.

We do not mean to suggest that no investments were made in clean production technology at that time. METI had established some standardized clean production technologies for adoption nationwide. One example is fuel conversion. To reduce sulfur dioxide, METI first required the use of crude oil with a low sulfur content and then liquid natural gas as a technical standard. But firms would not change fuels unless they could obtain a sufficient supply. METI negotiated with exporting countries to secure a supply that was adequate.

Since most clean production technologies are firm- or industry-specific in nature, a standard is difficult to establish. When it came to the reduction of mercury in wastewater from caustic-soda plants, METI designated the use of a technology called a diaphragm cell for producing caustic soda (instead of another technology, a mercury cell) as the technical standard, and a soft loan was provided for changing the production process. Despite the availability of soft loans, however, most of the firms did not readily change their system of production because of the high investment and operational costs involved. Once the mercury cell technology for producing caustic soda became available for use, firms readily adopted this new technology because of its cost advantage. Those firms that had employed the diaphragm cell had to invest twice in making a production change: once for the diaphragm cell technology and later for the mercury cell technology. They did not receive any compensation for METI's "misjudgment" concerning the appropriate technology.

Monitoring and Environmental Compliance

The dependence of the environmental soft loan program on the banking system should not be overlooked. The program will not have any beneficial impact on pollution unless the banking system can offer soft loans to the targeted polluters. Therefore, any financial institution, including public ones, should appraise the profitability of borrowers, analyze their cash flow, and evaluate collateral to ensure loan repayment.

Here there can be important differences in priorities. Loan repayment may weigh more than pollution prevention and vice versa. For instance, JDB and JFCSB attached more importance to repayment, while JEC emphasized pollution prevention. After providing the loan, JEC checked the firm's operational manual and the performance of the installed technology. None of the public financial institutions offering loans for pollution abatement investments monitored actual pollution levels.

Pollution, however, was reduced by a huge amount in Japan largely because of local governments' monitoring of discharges. Supported by residents, local governments enforced environmental regulations strictly, and sometimes they enacted ordinances that imposed more severe controls that those required by the central government. Moreover, a wider range of industrial plants was regulated. Firms had no choice but to comply with local governments' demands if they wanted to continue production in the same geographic area. In addition, there was a close collaboration between local governments and JEC: firms had to obtain approval from the prefectural government on their need to invest in the technology before applying for soft loans from JEC (Konishi 1996). Thus, strict enforcement by local governments prohibited firms from diverting the loan funds to other uses.

Financial Resources for the Environmental Soft Loan Program

The fourth feature of Japan's environmental soft loan program is its financing by the Fiscal Investment and Loan Program. When the government started pollution control, loan provisions were limited to certain types of industries located in the "heavily polluted area." As the pollution problem worsened in Japan in the 1960s and spread nationwide, and as more substances were identified as pollutants, the types of industries eligible for soft loans increased, and the area covered by environmental soft loan provisions widened. When a strict regulation was enacted and applied to all the industries in Japan, it created a huge demand for environmental soft loans. Without these loans, firms might delay the investment in pollution abatement because of the difficulty in obtaining financial resources. The Fiscal Investment and Loan Program enabled the public financial institutions to provide loans to meet the growing demand.

Every year public financial institutions can adjust the amount they borrow from the Fiscal Investment and Loan Program. They reduce their borrowing, for example, in years when the demand for soft loans declines. This has enabled the institutions to adjust to the fluctuations in demand without worsening their financial position.

The low-risk advantage gained by public financial institutions was nearly lost, however, when the market rate fell lower than the borrowing rate from the Fiscal Investment and Loan Program.

Public financial institutions are usually financed from the Fiscal Investment and Loan Program at a fixed interest rate with a fifteen-year repayment period, but they can extend loans with a repayment period of five to twenty years. This has enabled them to use the money from repaid loans to cover additional soft loans. The system works only when the market rate is higher than the institutions' borrowing rate.[6] But with financial deregulation and financial problems in the private sector, the market rate starting in the mid-1980s became lower than the borrowing rate. Public financial institutions saw the demand for soft loans decline. In principle, redemption before the scheduled repayment period was forbidden, which made the institutions' financial position worse.

After the enactment of waste management and recycling laws, demand for soft loans by waste disposal and recycling industries increased. The demand was high because commercial banks were reluctant to provide loans to these industries, especially the small ones without much collateral. The business risk in such industries can be high and the probability of default great. As a result, they are constrained in their attempt to achieve a balance between financial healthiness and pollution abatement.

Conclusion

We have already emphasized the connection between the strict environmental regulations and the provision of soft loans. However, even with this "package," the technology needed to implement pollution reduction measures would simply not have been available had it not been for the scientific and technical capacity in place in Japan after the rapid industrialization of the 1960s and early 1970s. Engineering personnel and scientific know-how available at the time provided the basis for technological breakthroughs in pollution control. In the case of developing countries, acquisition of this engineering and scientific capability would be essential, and related costs would have to be taken into account.

Monitoring plays a vital role in achieving successful implementation. In the case of Japan, local governments carry out this monitoring role very effectively. In developing countries, an important question to be resolved concerns compliance with environmental regulations and enforcement of them. A government ministry or office would need to be responsible for carrying out the monitoring and enforcement function.

In general, the soft loan package conflicts with the "polluter pays principle"and has two shortcomings. Firstly, it is inefficient. The cost of pollution control should be shouldered by the polluter. Secondly, from a moral aspect, the polluter ought to take sole responsibility for pollution abatement. However, when pollution has reached outrageous levels, soft loans are an effective means of achieving pollution reduction rapidly.

Lastly, how to raise funds to finance a soft loan program is a major question in developing countries. Japan has been fortunate to have sufficient financial resources to fund environmental incentives, but this is not the case in developing countries. Recent trends show that environmental taxes and/or charges are increasingly being used for this purpose in some countries.

Notes

1. Early repayment of soft loans was not an option for large firms, but it was sometimes possible for small and medium-size enterprises.

2. Although it may influence decisions about pollution abatement investments, environmental regulation is not included as an explanatory variable. This is because of technical difficulty in quantifying the regulation standard and also because its inclusion may result in collinearity problems with the soft loan variable.

3. The K-value regulation controlled above-ground sulfur dioxide concentration according to the height of the chimney. Between its enactment in 1968 and 1976, the K-value regulation was revised seven times in order to strengthen pollution control.

4. In fact, the information was supplied by one specialized public financial institution, JDB. Public financial institutions decided the amount of loan funds to borrow from the government for re-lending to firms, only after they had made an announcement to the public and had obtained responses from potential borrowers.

5. With respect to JDB's soft loans, the responsible government ministries conduct the de facto appraisal of technology. Firms are required to obtain a recommendation letter from the ministries when submitting loan applications (Konishi 1996).

6. JDB's lending rate was higher than its borrowing rate, even when applied to the environmental soft loan program. This enabled JDB to gain a big margin when it used repaid loans as a revolving fund to cover other loans. JEC, on the other hand, set the lending rate lower than its borrowing rate to provide financial resources for pollution prevention. The government, in turn, compensated JEC from the general budget for the loss of margin as well as for the appraisal cost. The financial burden to the government budget became heavier as the amount of the loan increased.

References

Janicke, Martin, and Helmut Weidner. 1995. *Successful Environmental Policy: A Critical Evaluation of Twenty-four Cases*. Berlin: Edition Sigma.

JDB (Japan Development Bank). various years. Business *Report of JDB* (in Japanese). Tokyo: JDB.

———. 1996. *Business Outline of JDB* (in Japanese). Tokyo: JDB.

JEC (Japan Environment Corporation). 1995. *Business Outline of JEC* (in Japanese). Tokyo: JEC.

———. 1996. *Business Statistics of JEC* (in Japanese). Tokyo: JEC.

JFCSB (Japan Financial Corporation for Small Business). 1996. *Business Statistics of JFCSB* (in Japanese). Tokyo: JFCSB.

Konishi, Aya. 1996. "Public Financial Programme for Pollution Prevention in Japan" (in Japanese). *Development Assistance Research* 3(1):168–87.

Lee, Soo Cheol. 1999. "Environmental Subsidies by Fiscal Investment and Loan in Japan" (in Japanese). *Research and Studies* 18: 30–48. Kyoto: Kyoto University Economic Society.

Matsuno, Yu. 1997. "How Effective Were Policy Instruments in Reducing Sulfur Oxide Emissions by Steel Mills in Japan?" (in Japanese). *The Economic Review* 159(5–6): 100–20. Kyoto: Kyoto University Economic Society.

Ministry of Finance. 1975-96. *Ministry of Finance Statistics Monthly* (in Japanese). Tokyo: Ministry of Finance.

Mori, Akihisa. 2002. "Industry and Water Management in Shiga Prefecture." *The Asian Journal of Biology Education* 1(1): 59–71.

6

The Link between Compliance at the Local Level and Global Environmental Goals: Waste Reduction Measures in Nagoya City

Kazuhiro Ueta

Global environmental issues have new features that are different from existing local environmental problems. In tackling the global issues, international cooperation is particularly important. Although each local community must cover the costs of addressing global environmental issues (global warming, for example), local communities do not directly realize all the resulting benefits, since they tend to be spread on a global scale. Yet antipollution measures taken by local communities are often implemented without any acknowledgment of their effects on conservation of the global environment. In fact, measures taken to protect the global environment often improve the quality of the local environment, and measures taken for the local environment help conserve the global environment. This "synergy effect" must be considered in the decisionmaking process at the local level. Measures to mitigate global warming tend to be viewed as irrelevant by local governments, but they can and should be linked to the specific needs of local communities for a cleaner and safer environment.

This chapter explores the connection between local environmental actions and the global environment by focusing on the issue of waste disposal in Nagoya City, Japan. Alarmed by its inability to secure sites for final disposal of its wastes, Nagoya City implemented effective measures to reduce and recycle them. The chapter attempts to assess as quantitatively as possible the cost-effectiveness of waste reduction and recycling measures. This chapter also assesses the implications of these local efforts on global warming. Nagoya City's successful experience in waste reduction is discussed in terms of its synergy effect.

Overview of the Waste Reduction Issue in Japan

More than thirty years have passed since the waste disposal crisis in Japan was identified, yet few examples of success in waste reduction can be cited. This is mainly because Japan's mass waste–producing society has developed without adequate attention given to this critical issue. The need for waste reduction has not been sufficiently integrated into national policymaking with regard to production, consumption, urban development, and national land reform. A drastic reform of the social structure has not been achieved. By and large, the Japanese government has regarded the production of a massive amount of waste as a given. Disposing of wastes, rather than reducing wastes, has been the focus.

Since the Meiji Era, Japan has favored incineration as the method of waste disposal, and for many years waste disposal has been regarded as a domestic problem. But waste incineration emits a considerable amount of carbon dioxide, and therefore it has an impact on global warming.

The Waste Problem in Nagoya City

The need in Nagoya City of final disposal sites for urban wastes ("general waste" in terms of law) has a long history, but the waste disposal problem did not become pronounced until 1992. Then, it was not until the late 1990s that waste disposal was recognized as a citywide problem. By 1996 the amount of wastes generated in Nagoya City had become alarmingly high: one million tons per year compared with approximately 840,000 tons in 1985.

Today domestic refuse makes up 70 percent of the total amount of wastes generated in Nagoya. As lifestyles changed, domestic refuse grew to include not only kitchen wastes but also disposable goods, plastic containers, and packaging materials, making the disposal of the wastes increasingly difficult.

Wastes generated in Nagoya are either combustible (general waste) or noncombustible (source-segregated refuse that is collected). The combustible refuse is incinerated at four incineration plants in the city. Most of the noncombustible wastes are recycled or compacted to reduce volume at waste processing plants.

For the incineration ash generated in Nagoya City, the city constructed a final disposal site in Tajimi City in the Gifu Prefecture. After that, little landfill capacity in the area remained. The Waste Disposal and Public Cleaning Law affirmed the "Principle of Disposal of Refuse within the Boundaries of Each Ward." Therefore, Nagoya City had to locate the next final disposal site for its wastes within its *own* borders.

The Fujimae tidal flat, a territorial sea of Fujimae, Minato-ku, at West One in Nagoya Port, was proposed as the next large-scale site. However, the Fujimae tidal flat is famous both domestically and internationally for being a habitat for migratory birds. (The area recently became a registered wetlands under the Ramsar Convention.) Nagoya City was publicly criticized for its plan to use a tidal flat as a landfill without first making efforts to reduce wastes. Local residents and environmental conservation groups protested. In the end, Nagoya City abandoned its plan to build a new waste disposal facility in the Fujimae tidal flat.

In February 1999 Nagoya City declared a state of emergency for waste disposal and presented a concrete plan to reduce waste by 200,000 tons or 20 percent in two years. With the support of local residents, the city expanded the area for collecting cans and bottles from nine wards to all sixteen wards in the city. Citizens who voluntarily collected wastes received a subsidy. In order to make each citizen more aware of the waste he or she generated, the city changed its collection policies. Collection by container at each apartment complex was abolished. Waste service companies stopped accepting industrial wastes (such as used papers, cans, and bottles) for disposal in municipal facilities. Instead they started charging a dumping fee.

Waste Reduction in Nagoya City

Figure 6.1 shows the amount of waste disposed of in municipal facilities in Nagoya City in fiscal years 1998, 1999, and 2000. In fiscal year 2000, the amount of disposed wastes was adjusted to exclude the disaster refuse generated by the Tokai torrential rains.

Figure 6.2 classifies the waste disposed of in Nagoya City by type: combustible refuse, noncombustible refuse, bulky wastes collected by the city, wastes collected by beautification campaign workers, recyclable wastes, and garbage voluntarily collected by citizens. The amount of combustible refuse drastically decreased in Nagoya City from 1998 to 2000. Because of strict controls on separate collection, waste formerly disposed of as combustible refuse was collected as recyclable waste.

In fiscal year 1998 the amount of recyclable waste collected in Nagoya City was only 18,001 tons; by 2000 this amount had tripled to 56,594 tons (see Figure 6.3). Recyclable wastes include collected bottles, cans, plastic containers, and paper cartons. Recyclable wastes that are collected

Figure 6.1 *Waste Disposal Amount in Nagoya City*

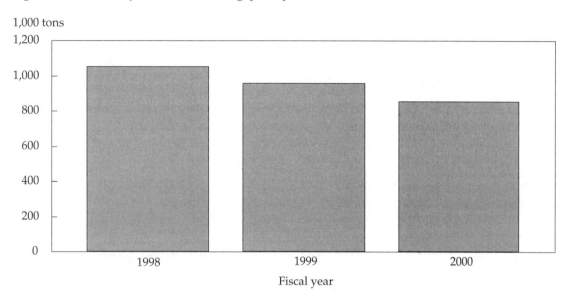

Source: Unpublished Nagoya City data compiled by the author.

later at the time of intermediate processing are not included in Figure 6.3. (If bulky waste and noncombustible waste after the intermediate processing are collected as recyclable waste, the total amount of collected recyclable waste would increase from 280,000 tons in 1998[1] to 380,000 tons in 1999 and 650,000 tons in 2000, or an increase of 40 percent and 70 percent, respectively.)

Recyclable waste collected voluntarily and solely by citizens (see Figure 6.4) is primarily waste paper in three general categories: (1) newspapers and fliers; (2) magazines, books, notebooks,

Figure 6.2 *Amount of Waste Disposal in Nagoya City, by Type of Waste*

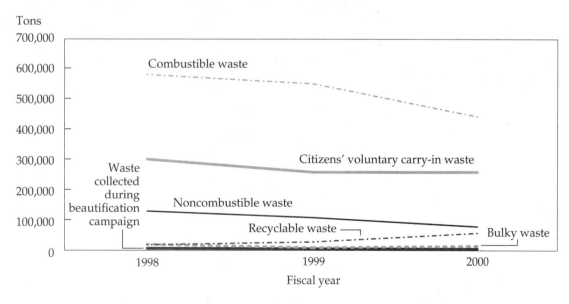

Note: The category "Citizens' voluntary carry-in waste" includes all types of waste brought in voluntarily by citizens' groups.
Source: Unpublished Nagoya City data compiled by the author.

Figure 6.3 *Resource Recovery in Nagoya City*

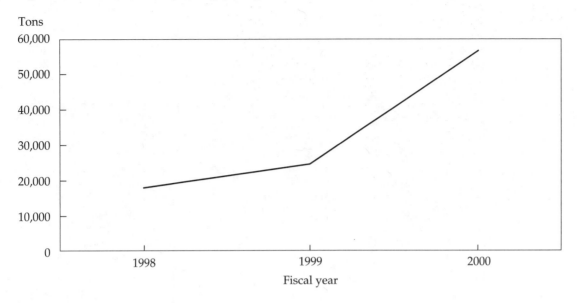

Source: Unpublished Nagoya City data compiled by the author.

catalogues, calendars, paper files, copy papers, memo pads, and envelopes; and (3) cardboards. In Japan waste paper is collected by Parent-Teacher Association groups, children's groups, citizens' groups that bring the waste paper to recycling centers, and private carriers who bring waste paper in to their factories. In 2000 a new method of group collection of waste paper was begun—the "school district consultation method." This method is really a citizens' cooperative approach organized by school districts. News distributors and private carriers were also asked to assist.

Figure 6.4 *Amount of Recyclable Waste Collected by Citizens Voluntarily in Nagoya City*

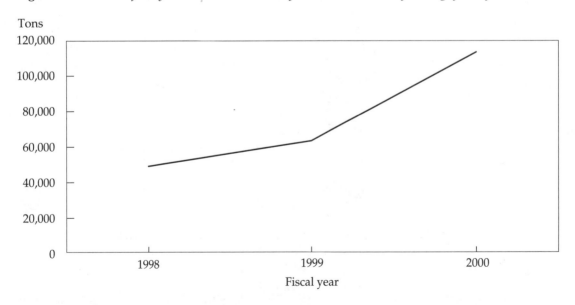

Source: Unpublished Nagoya City data compiled by the author.

Although the activities are regarded as citizens' voluntary waste collection, they can also be valued as administrative efforts for resource recovery, since the city of Nagoya gives subsidies for the group collection and the collection at recycle stations.

The amount of landfill (including incineration ash and noncombustibles) decreased by half from 280,000 tons in 1998 to 120,000 tons in 2000. Additionally, there were 30,000 tons of incineration ash reclaimed by private companies in 2000. This raised the total to 150,000 tons, which still is approximately half of the amount reclaimed in 1998.

Several factors contributed to the reduction in final waste disposal shown in Figure 6.5: an increase in recyclable kitchen waste, intensified voluntary collection, promotion of industrial waste recycling, and a tolling system for industrial refuse. (General wastes in Japan are classified as either domestic wastes from households or industry refuse other than the refuse specified as industrial solid wastes generated by business establishments, such as retail stores.) Industry refuse declined by 23 percent from 435,000 tons in 1998 to 335,000 tons in 2000. This contributed greatly to the reduction of the final disposal amount.

Nagoya City succeeded in achieving a large-scale reduction of wastes. The process of waste disposal in the city changed remarkably after the declaration of a state of emergency in 1999 (see Figures 6.6 and 6.7). Particularly noteworthy is the improved collection of separate wastes in Nagoya City.

Types of Waste and the Treatment Process

Currently in Nagoya, combustibles are collected twice a week at every door, and noncombustibles are collected once a week at collection stations (see Table 6.1). Both kinds of waste are put in transparent garbage bags designated by the city. Recyclable wastes (such as bottles and cans) that were not collected separately are now collected once a week at the stations. Plastic bottles, containers, and packaging materials (both in paper and plastic) are collected separately and reclassified after the intermediate processing.

Figure 6.5 *Final Waste Disposal in Nagoya City, Including Citizens' Voluntary Collection*

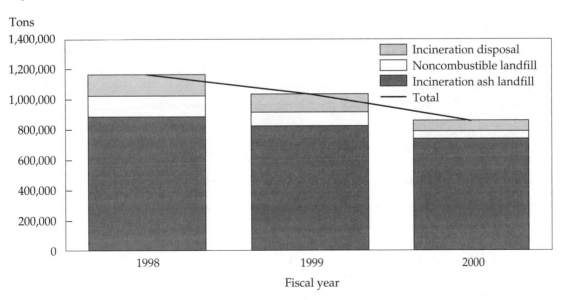

Source: Unpublished Nagoya City data compiled by the author.

Figure 6.6 *Treatment of General Waste in Nagoya City, 1998*
(tons)

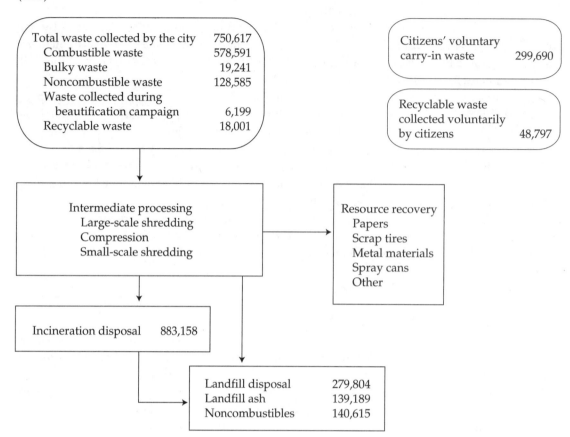

Source: Unpublished Nagoya City data compiled by the author.

Separate collection began in 2000. The result is a 20 percent decrease in waste disposal, a threefold increase in the amount of recyclables collected, and a 50 percent reduction in the amount of final landfill disposal. The capacity of Aigi landfill in Tajimi was 580,000 tons at the end of fiscal year 2000, and there is a plan to prepare additional space for 590,000 tons. Nagoya City succeeded in fulfilling its original objective to save the tidal flat. Now let us consider what effect these local improvements in waste disposal have had on global warming.

Waste Reduction and Reduction of Greenhouse Gases

Quantification of Greenhouse Gas Emissions

Attempts have been made to quantify greenhouse gas emissions, especially carbon dioxide emissions. In a lifecycle assessment (LCA) of a solid waste management system, CO_2 emissions are calculated as part of the system's environmental load. It is theoretically possible to quantify the amount of CO_2 emitted at each stage of waste disposal (that is, waste collection, intermediate processing, incineration disposal, recycling, and landfill disposal).

Local governments as well as individual firms conduct lifecycle assessments. Considerable ambiguities arise in efforts to evaluate carbon dioxide emissions. For instance, recyclable waste collection and intermediate processing are conducted both by Nagoya City and by private companies,

Figure 6.7 *Treatment of General Waste in Nagoya City, 2000*
(tons)

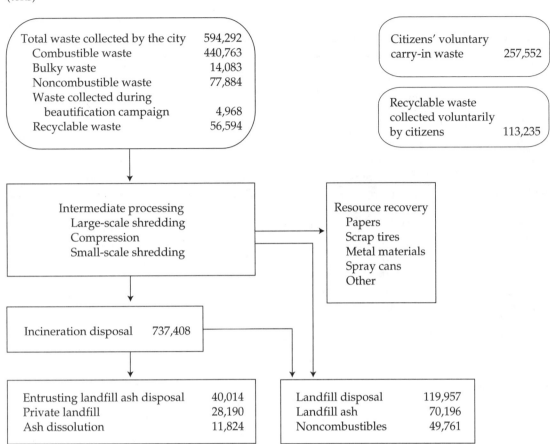

but the city government does not keep track of the results of private sector efforts to recycle. Even in cases when the city government does know the amount of waste recycled by private companies, city officials do not have the data to calculate the amount of CO_2 emitted by the recyclable wastes generated within Nagoya City. This is because the private companies also collect recyclables from outside the city.

Given the difficulty of making correct assessments, this chapter attempts to quantify the amount of CO_2 emissions by relying only on information disclosed by Nagoya City. It assesses (1) the amount of CO_2 emitted in the "public process of waste disposal" and (2) the amount of CO_2 emissions reduced through waste reduction measures. "Public process of waste disposal" basically refers to the wastes collected by the city. As for the wastes brought in voluntarily by citizens, only the greenhouse gas emissions (GHGs) from intermediate processing, incineration disposal, and landfill disposal are included in the calculation; GHGs generated in transportation of wastes collected by citizens are not included.

Energy Consumption Necessary for a Ton of Waste Disposal

The amount of energy consumed to dispose of one ton of waste is calculated by quantifying the CO_2 emissions generated in the process. Figure 6.8 compares data for 1998, when separated

Table 6.1 *Waste Collection in Nagoya City, by Waste Category*

Category	1998	1999	2000
Wastes			
Combustibles	■ Twice a week	■ Twice a week	■ Twice a week
Noncombustibles	● Once a week	● Once a week	● Once a week
Bulky wastes	■ Once a month (on application basis, charged)	■ Once a month (on application basis, charged)	■ Once a month (on application basis, charged)
Spray cans	—	—	● Once a week
Resources			
Cans	● Once a week (9 wards)	● Once a week (whole city)	● Once a week (whole city)
Bottles	● Once a week (9 wards)	● Once a week (whole city)	● Once a week (whole city)
Paper cartons	▲ 300 points + elementary and junior high schools	▲ 300 points + elementary and junior high schools	▲ 300 points + elementary and junior high schools
PET bottles	▲ 300 points + elementary and junior high schools	▲ 300 points + elementary and junior high schools	▲ Once in every two weeks
Paper containers	—	—	● Once in every two weeks
Plastic containers	—	—	● Once in every two weeks
Button type batteries	▲ 200 points + elementary and junior high schools	▲ 200 points + elementary and junior high schools	▲ 200 points + elementary and junior high schools

■ Collection at every door (station collection in some areas).
● Station collection (local dumping place, one in 50–60 households).
▲ Collection at designated points (collection boxes set at grocery stores and public facilities).
Source: Unpublished Nagoya City data compiled by the author.

collection had not yet been introduced, to data for 2000, after separated collection had begun. The amount of CO_2 emissions is smaller for all categories of waste: combustible waste, noncombustible waste, bulky waste, waste collected during the beautification campaign, citizens' voluntary carry-in waste, and resource recovery waste.

The more intermediate processing is conducted, the more energy is required for transportation, shredding, and compaction of wastes. After the declaration of a "garbage emergency" in Nagoya City, the city began serious efforts to reduce the amount of waste for final disposal as landfill. Its reforms increased the amount of energy used per ton of waste disposal because separated collection and intermediate processing expended more energy. The total amount of energy consumed in the whole process of waste disposal declined, however, because Nagoya City succeeded in reducing by half the total amount of waste that was generated.

Figure 6.9 shows the amount of CO_2 emissions generated in six stages of waste disposal: collection, transportation, separation, shredding, landfill disposal, and dissolution of incinerator ash. CO_2 emissions generated by incineration are shown in Figure 6.10. These emissions are incredibly large compared to emissions from collection, transportation, separation, shredding, landfill disposal, and dissolution. The total amount of CO_2 emissions generated by the waste disposal process from start to finish is shown in Figure 6.11.

Figure 6.8 *Energy Consumed to Dispose of a Ton of Waste in Nagoya City*

Kilograms of carbon dioxide per one ton of waste

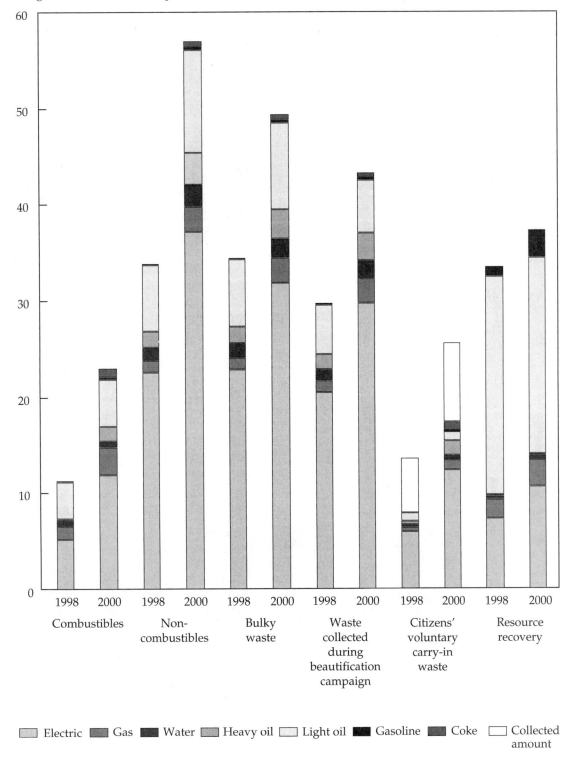

Source: Unpublished Nagoya City data compiled by the author.

Figure 6.9 *CO_2 Emissions per Ton of Waste, by Disposal Process in Nagoya City* (excluding incineration process)

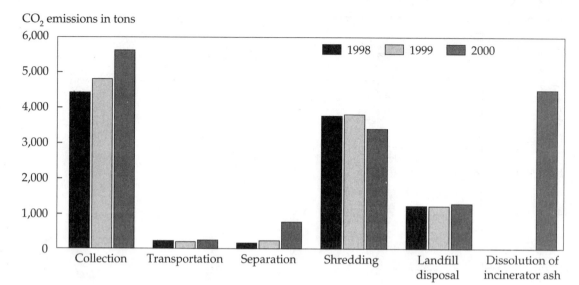

Source: Unpublished Nagoya City data compiled by the author.

Nagoya City's drastic measures for waste reduction increased the amount of CO_2 emissions associated with the process of waste collection and processing described above by approximately 1,500 tons annually (6,000 tons per year if dissolution is included) within two years (1998-2000). However, as the city significantly lowered the amount of wastes for incineration through waste reduction measures, CO_2 emitted during the incineration process decreased by more than 60,000

Figure 6.10 *CO_2 Emissions in Incineration Process*

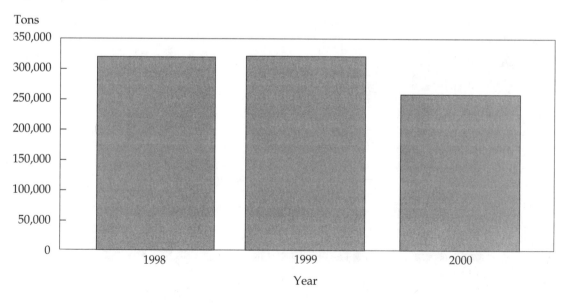

Source: Unpublished Nagoya City data compiled by the author.

Figure 6.11 *Total Amount of CO_2 Emissions Generated by Waste Disposal Process in Nagoya City*

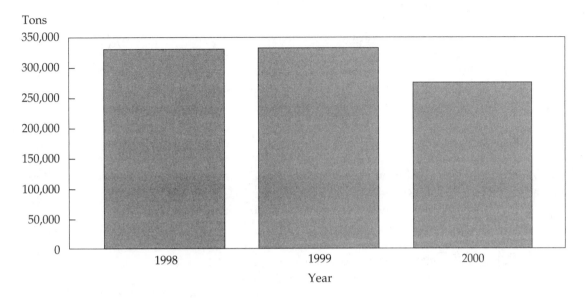

Note: Total emissions from 1998 to 2000 declined by about 55,000 tons.
Source: Unpublished Nagoya City data compiled by the author.

tons per year, as shown in Figure 6.10. (Incineration accounts for the largest share of CO_2 emissions for the entire waste disposal process.) Consequently, the amount CO_2 emissions for the whole process of waste disposal was reduced by 55,000 tons (see Figure 6.11).

The delay in building a new final disposal site (a delay made possible by Nagoya City's waste reduction measures) "saved" CO_2 emissions. Carbon dioxide would have been released in the process of building the site. If this effect is included, the waste reduction measures would have lowered emissions even more, further mitigating global warming.

Costs of Waste Disposal

Nagoya City calculates the cost of waste disposal per ton. First, it determines the cost accounting period on an account year basis. Total departmental expenditures during the cost accounting period are compiled based on the settlement of accounts of annual spending on environmental projects. Next, departmental costs on the waste disposal process are computed. Finally, the aggregated costs of public collection and voluntary collection are separately determined.

The *Annual Report, 2000* released by Nagoya City's Environmental Affairs Bureau classifies waste disposal costs in several categories. Personnel costs include wages, benefits for employees other than retirement benefits, and mutual aid money, all of which are included in the annual budget.

Nonpersonal expenditures do not include depreciation costs and the interest paid on bond issues. The costs for land acquisition also are not included. Costs that are inappropriate for annual expenditure, such as expenditure on outsourcing the design of new facilities, are deferred as a cost element to the next fiscal year.

Depreciation costs are calculated separately for buildings, facilities, work pieces, and vehicles. The cost elements are the construction fee recognized as capital expenditure, and the equipment costs necessary for purchasing vehicles. The depreciation period is fifty years for reinforced concrete buildings, thirty years for wooden structures, fifteen years for facilities and work pieces, and five years for vehicles, in accordance with the straight-line method of depreciation. The interest on bond issues includes the interest payments for the bonds issued to raise funds for building facilities.

Figure 6.12 shows the costs of waste disposal in Nagoya City in 1998, 1999, and 2000. Expenditures in 2000 were bigger than in the previous two years. One reason is nonrecurring expenditure items, such as construction and maintenance of waste disposal facilities and landfill sites. They are included in Figure 6.13 as facility expenses for environmental projects.

Cost-Effectiveness of Waste Reduction Measures

As noted at the beginning of the chapter, there is a synergistic relationship between local measures to reduce carbon dioxide emissions and the global environment. Specifically, waste reduction at the local level mitigates global warming. Figure 6.14 depicts this synergistic relationship by tracking three factors from 1998 to 2000: waste reduction in Nagoya City as a result of local policy measures; the costs of implementing the local policy measures; and the reduction of CO_2 emissions as a consequence of local policy. The total amount of waste disposal (as shown in Figure 6.1) decreased by 20 percent from 1,050,307 tons in 1998 to 851,844 tons in 2000. Although the cost of waste disposal increased from 43.4 billion yen in 1998 to 47.4 billion yen in 2000, CO_2 emissions declined by 55,000 tons. The costs of waste reduction in 2000 would have been much higher if the time and effort required for waste separation had been valuated and included in the total (an undertaking beyond the scope of this chapter).

Figure 6.12 *Costs of Waste Disposal in Nagoya City*

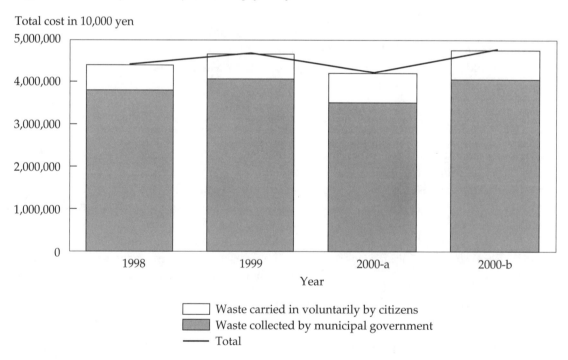

Note: The graph for 2000-a shows the cost of waste disposal excluding 56,594 tons of collected recyclables. The 2000-b graph includes the 56,594 tons. The 2000-b data are also used for analyzing policy cost-effectiveness, since waste recycling can be regarded as a municipal policy measure for waste reduction.
Source: Unpublished Nagoya City data compiled by the author.

Figure 6.13 *Annual Costs for Environmental Projects in Nagoya City*

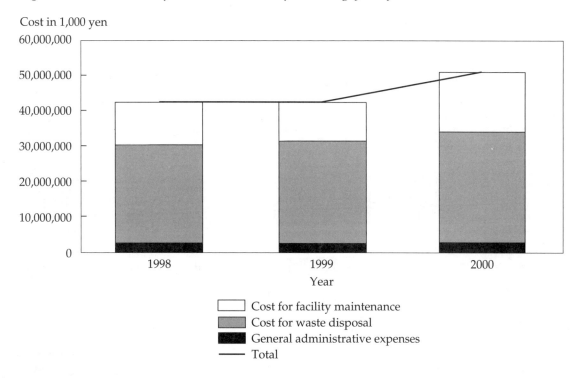

Source: Unpublished Nagoya City data compiled by the author.

Figure 6.14 *Synergistic Relationship between Local and Global Effects*

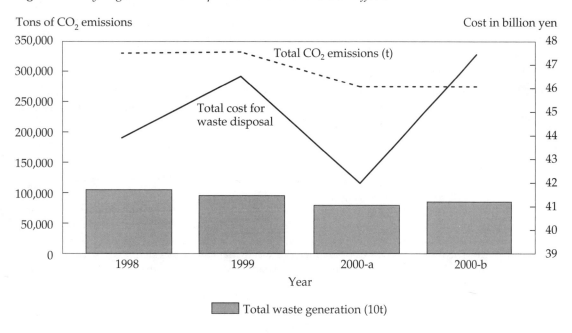

Note: See Figure 6.12 for an explanation of the year 2000 data.
Source: Unpublished Nagoya City data compiled by the author.

Since the additional 4 billion yen resulted in the reduction of 198,463 tons of wastes, the cost of waste reduction can be estimated as 20,200 yen per ton. If the total cost of waste disposal is divided by the amount of disposed wastes, the unit cost is about 41,800 yen per ton for the year 1998 and about 55,600 yen per ton for 2000.

A carbon tax is being considered in Japan. The monetary value of the reduced 55,000 tons of CO_2 emissions can be calculated with reference to this proposed tax. The benefits of CO_2 emissions reduction would be about 165 million yen if the price of one ton of CO_2 is 3,000 yen. Assuming that Nagoya City implemented waste reduction measures to reduce CO_2 emissions, the cost-benefit ratio between the costs required for waste reduction measures (C_R) and the benefits of the abatement of CO_2 emissions (B_A) would be approximately 0.41. This means that $B_A - C_R < 0$, and the measures would not be worth implementing.

The starting point of Nagoya City's waste reduction efforts was its inability to secure a new site for final disposal of its wastes. If the landfill site had been constructed, the costs would have been approximately 25 billion yen. The city may still need to construct this site, but such a necessity has clearly been postponed by its efforts to reduce waste. Assuming that the life of a waste disposal facility is forty years and the amount of final waste disposal can be reduced by 20 percent through waste reduction measures, 6.25 billion yen can be cut from the costs of constructing the waste disposal facility.

Therefore, since the benefit of postponing the construction of a disposal site by waste reduction (B_D) can be estimated at 6.25 billion yen, the benefit-cost ratio (B_D/C_R) is approximately 1.56. This means that $B_D - C_R > 0$, and implementation of the measures is economically justified.

In and of themselves, Nagoya City's waste reduction measures are rewarding. If their ancillary benefits are considered (that is, the benefits of reducing CO_2 emissions), the benefit-cost ratio ($(B_D + B_A)/C_R$) increases to 1.98. This suggests that measures to conserve the local environment can mitigate global warming to an important extent. Priority should be given to implementing waste reduction measures that benefit the local environment, have a high benefit-cost ratio, and reduce CO_2 emissions. Even if the benefit-cost ratio (B_D/C_R) of a measure or project for local environment conservation is smaller than 1, the total benefit-cost ratio if ancillary benefits (B_A) are included ($(B_D + B_A)/C_R$) may be larger than 1; therefore the measure should be implemented. However, the ancillary benefits would not belong to the agents that implement the measures or projects. In other words, the benefits would be global not local. Therefore, the measures or projects would not be implemented without some kind of inducement. The global community needs to explore certain institutions in order to fill this gap.

The benefits of waste reduction in Nagoya City are not limited to postponement of the construction of a final disposal site. Because the Fujimae tidal flat was spared when the city gave up its plans to construct a landfill site, an ecologically important tidal flat was saved.

Note

1. The 280,000 tons is the total of all recycled waste. This includes "first level" recycling (that is, sorted out bottles, cans, plastic bottles, paper) and "second level" recycling (for example, pulverized large plastic materials and scrap metal for re-use). To help readers better understand waste processing, a few general comments follow. The municipal waste stream includes waste that can be recycled. Wastes that cannot be recycled go either to the incinerator or to the landfill. Most combustibles are incinerated. Regarding the recyclable waste stream, this includes waste items that are collected and separated early in the waste processing/disposal cycle (the first level of recycling referred to above). At a later stage of processing, a greater amount of recyclables are recovered (for example, large items of disposed materials, such as scrap metal, construction wood and boards, wood and plastic furniture).

7

Conclusion: Lessons Learned on the Importance of Local Initiatives

Adriana Bianchi, Wilfrido Cruz, and Masahisa Nakamura

Although many developing countries recognize the severity of their environmental problems, they have had difficulty designing environmental regulations and ensuring their compliance. The underlying theme of this book is the catalytic role local initiatives can play in these efforts. Local initiatives include actions by local governments, community groups, and private industry, and they form an important complement to environmental management efforts that may otherwise emphasize only the role of the central government and environmental agencies.

During the reconstruction period after the Second World War and the rapid industrial growth in the 1960s and 1970s, a wide range of local initiatives was successfully applied to the serious pollution problems in Japanese communities. The case studies highlight relevant examples for developing countries, including the development of air and water pollution management approaches and the supporting role that can be played by economic incentives and global environmental goals.

The Main Components of Local Approaches in Japan

Environmental regulation and compliance in Japan have been described in this book in terms of specific local pollution problems and specific responses by communities and factories to address them. Contributing to effective environmental regulation and compliance are the following components of the Japanese experience:

- the sustained involvement of local authorities in determining environmental regulations and ensuring compliance
- the influence of community-based constituencies and the willingness of private industry to cooperate with local management efforts
- the availability of technology and the strengthening of management capacity to respond to specific environmental problems
- the presence of favorable economic conditions and financial support to industry for pollution abatement activities.

The process of developing local regulations and enforcement mechanisms in the 1960s and 1970s was begun as a result of several factors. The most important were an increase in awareness by community residents of the seriousness of the local pollution problem and the subsequent responsiveness of local government units (LGUs). The development of pollution control regulations and their effective implementation were aided by the business or industry culture in Japan: firms identify closely with the communities in which they are located. Lastly, financial incentives and favorable economic conditions were instrumental, especially in helping private industry invest in more efficient (waste-reducing) technology in general and in pollution control equipment in particular.

The Relevance of Japan's Experience to Developing Countries: Local and National Implications

At first sight, Japan's experience with pollution control may not appear relevant to countries with a very different history, not only in terms of industrial development and income levels, but also in terms of social and cultural characteristics. However, many of the changes occurring now in developing countries mirror changes that occurred in Japan in the period of rapid reconstruction and re-industrialization during the 1960s and 1970s.

The case studies from Japan are relevant to developing countries because they present practical alternatives to traditional approaches that rely heavily on central government interventions. The case studies describe local approaches that involve local businesses and community organizations as well as city governments in efforts to control pollution. Japan's experience also is relevant in terms of the social and informal factors that improved factories' compliance with environmental regulations. The Japanese experience could be valuable as a model for using similar (if less potent) factors in developing countries where formal enforcement methods are often undermined by governmental inefficiency or political interference.

Developing-country reviewers noted significant differences between Japan and developing countries in Asia with regard to the timing of industrial growth and the capacities and practices of industries. (Please refer to the Introduction and Appendix for the summary of reviews.) Nevertheless, the reviewers recognized the efficacy of promoting local approaches to pollution management in developing countries. Useful models from Japan could help improve local initiatives elsewhere. The wide range of air and water pollution problems presented in the case studies was considered especially instructive. The varied circumstances that are described can help developing-country officials and leaders in the private sector recognize the potential of specific approaches, depending on community conditions and existing partnerships. Since local approaches must be tailored closely to local conditions, it is particularly important that developing-country officials and local leaders be flexible and receptive to local factors that may be unique in their communities.

In Japan local approaches to environmental compliance vary by community, depending on its level of awareness of local pollution problems and the types of local partnerships that can be formed. For example, the use of pollution control agreements (PCAs) is now widespread in Japan, with thousands currently in force. However, in the early period of pollution management, Japanese cities took somewhat different approaches. In Yokohama, pollution control agreements between industries and the local government played the key role in determining pollution management targets and in setting up systems of monitoring and enforcement. By contrast, in Kitakyushu, a more direct approach was taken; the local government developed pollution regulations primarily through informal but effective "administrative guidance" of industry's environmental practices. In between these two examples is the case of Osaka. In Osaka traditional cooperation between the city government and local businesses made a partnership approach to pollution reduction the logical and practical one.

By developing a solid constituency for environmental management, local initiatives can also provide a more solid foundation for national policies. In Japan local governments built a broad constituency for pollution control that later spurred changes in environmental policy at the national level. The process was gradual. After the Second World War a national antipollution law was effectively blocked from being introduced into the Diet by business interests. Later, when a national law was eventually passed in 1967, its impact was undermined by explicit requirements to preserve "harmony" between industrial growth and pollution control. However, by the 1970s, support had grown for strong national legislation on pollution control. Communities and local governments had won such broad endorsement for antipollution programs that even political processes at the national level were significantly affected. Favorable court decisions on pollution-related cases added momentum to the drive to pass a national bill. Traditional politicians recognized that they could lose voters to other parties supporting pollution control platforms, and this led to changes in their policy positions. In time a strong national pollution control law was passed.

The Role of Social Responsibility

As the case studies indicate, social responsibility or social pressure to help the public good plays a significant role in Japan. Of course, businesses in Japan want to increase their profitability, and some businesses have strongly opposed pollution regulations. In general, however, Japanese businesses appear to be very mindful of their social role in the community. One example is RK Excel, a metal-plating company that produces automobile and motorcycle parts. As the case study makes clear, cultural factors played an important role in convincing the company to reduce water pollution. Once its responsibility for the local chemical problem was established, RK Excel went to great lengths to ameliorate it.

RK Excel's environmental program was mainly motivated by a desire to maintain the company's good standing in Yagura town. The pollution control program adopted by RK Excel was far more stringent than the basic pollution control requirements of the 1970 law. Indeed, RK Excel's pollution control agreement is far stricter than most PCAs. Environmental management represents more than 4 percent of the company's annual production budget.

Pollution control efforts in Lake Biwa also illustrate how social responsibility has influenced compliance with environmental regulations by Japanese businesses. When the Shiga prefecture imposed restrictions on water pollutants, there was general cooperation at the local level. Nevertheless, cases of noncompliance with discharge regulations occurred. In addressing the problem of noncompliance, the local government approached the enforcement of regulations governing toxic and nontoxic pollutants differently. If effluents contained toxic pollutants, there was very strict and direct regulation by the local government. However, more flexibility was allowed with regard to nontoxic pollutants, and the approach depended more on social pressure.

The local pollution authorities undertook regular spot inspections as a means of monitoring noncompliance. When noncompliance was spotted, a light warning was usually issued to the offending party. Often this approach worked because the business would respond to the informal social pressure to change its polluting practices and clean up the environment. Light warnings, however, did not resolve all problems. In some cases a stern warning was required, and if that went unheeded there was the potential use of administrative actions. This means of enforcement was rarely needed to ensure compliance.

As noted by the developing country reviewers, polluting companies' sense of social responsibility may be less in developing countries than in Japan. The model of using social pressures to achieve compliance might be adapted in these countries by increasing the visibility of polluters, thereby increasing the social pressures that could be applied. By advertising the polluting activities of individual factories and thus increasing public awareness, developing countries could increase the potential for action.

In Indonesia the national government helped to determine the responsibility of individual factories for pollution. Indonesia's Program for Pollution Control, Evaluation, and Rating (PROPER) called for the assignment of pollution "colors" to polluters. The worst polluters were classified as "black," while those complying with environmental regulations or exceeding those requirements were elevated to a "gold" classification. In between the extremes of "black" and "gold" were different levels of pollution classified in a variety of colors. Similar attempts have been made in other countries in the region, and they appear to have effectively increased the visibility of polluters' actions and concomitantly the social pressures on them to reduce pollution.

Although this approach was not directly part of the Japanese experience, it depends on social responsibility and local perceptions to increase compliance with environmental regulations. Thus, this "color-coding" system could be useful elsewhere if it is incorporated within a program of promoting compliance through local government and community action, and in partnership with the specific industries.

The Role of Special Financing

In Japan soft loans help businesses invest in measures to remediate pollution and introduce cleaner processes. Just as Japanese businesses appear to be more willing than businesses in developing countries to accept social responsibility to protect the environment, public institutions in Japan appear to be more willing to provide incentives to soften the financial burden of compliance with environmental regulations.

The introduction of the soft loan program was linked to the enactment of pollution control legislation. Before the 1970s, polluters were not fully aware of the social cost of pollution, and therefore soft loans were a needed incentive. A later stage of the incentive program linked soft loans to the standardization of cleaner technology. The program helped companies meet the standards, and it helped in the development of a new clean-technology industry.

In the early days, special financing for investment in environmental protection was noteworthy not only because of the subsidized rate (although the rate was a significant incentive), but because it made financing for the new priorities available for many businesses that otherwise would not have been able to get such financing from traditional sources, such as local banks. At that time investments in efforts to control pollution would not have been particularly "bankable" since the investments did not lead directly to immediate improvements in revenues.

When discussing the relevance to developing countries of Japan's financial incentives approach, developing country reviewers highlighted three issues: how the approach would fit in with current views on the Polluter Pays Principle (PPP); how local initiatives could enhance financial incentives; and lastly how financing to improve the global environment could assist local initiatives.

The use of special financing to control pollution in Japan predated discussions of the PPP, a key principle associated with environmental management incentives. As the reviewers noted, the soft loan or financing approach used in Japan appears to run counter to the Polluter Pays Principle. In recent years the PPP has gained increasing acceptance among both national and international environmental agencies. The value of PPP is that the social cost of pollution is clearly assigned to the source. In fact, the cost of cleanup or prevention is viewed as the responsibility of the source, so that in general subsidized financing for anti-pollution investment is not appropriate. However, the reviewers als recognized the need for a proactive approach to specific pollution control problems. The main concern was how to respond quickly to serious pollution problems. Thus, the practical test for an approach was whether it could provide timely help to control these special problems, could be well targeted, and the need for incentives would decline over time.

The distinctive implementation feature of the soft loan program in Japan was its close tie to many local initiatives. Thus, the burden of monitoring the productivity of the loan for the financing agencies was greatly reduced by LGU oversight. Especially in the early period, there was very close cooperation between the financing agencies (such as the Japan Environment Corporation, the Japan Development Bank, and the Japan Financial Corporation for Small Business) and local government units. For their part, the LGUs were very supportive of the soft loan program because it made possible immediate compliance with the new pollution control agreements. This feature of special financing in Japan (namely, the close ties to local initiatives) could be useful to many developing countries in their efforts to improve the efficiency of their financial incentive programs.

Lastly, the example of solid waste management in Nagoya City demonstrated the link between local initiatives and global environmental goals. Financial incentives not only promote local and national efforts to reduce pollution. They may also support local initiatives that contribute to the achievement of global goals. The high visibility of global environmental issues in Japan followed the climate change meeting in Kyoto in 1997. Local actions to reduce pollution can have ancillary benefits, as the case study on solid waste management in Nagoya City explains. Congested metropolitan areas in the region are producing levels of solid waste that are rapidly multiplying. Landfill areas are becoming limited, and incineration of solid waste may become more common, with negative implications for greenhouse gas emissions. In addition, the need to open up new landfills may also affect wetland habitats and coastal marine resources around many large cities in the region. This could lead to increased impact on biodiversity and international water resources.

Improved Cooperation with Local Industry and Government Agencies: A Look to the Future

This book has focused on the role of community actions and local governments in Japan and the potential for implementing similar initiatives in developing countries. Two related aspects contributing to effective enforcement and compliance approaches were also mentioned as part of the Japanese experience, namely the close cooperation of private industry and government agencies with environmental management efforts at the community or municipal level. These aspects have not received as much attention in developing countries, and they would be useful components in the agenda for future environmental action.

In Japan it is clear that local communities, including municipal governments and community organizations, were able to work closely with individual industries and industry associations to identify environmental regulation targets that were practical for local conditions and to cooperate in monitoring and enforcement activities. Of course, Japanese industries tried to avoid responsibility for pollution in the early phase of rapid industrial growth and during the introduction of environmental regulation. However, once regulations were imposed or consensus on the need to control pollution was reached with local government and community organizations, there was close cooperation between communities and local industry.

In developing countries in East Asia, important steps in this direction are the national government projects on pollution information disclosure. By revealing the air, water, and solid waste pollution records of individual factories, some of these projects have motivated industry to adopt pollution abatement programs. For example, this approach was highlighted in the discussion of Indonesian and Philippine experiences. An important next step would be to develop specific pollution abatement programs directly with the industries involved. Japan's experience in the use of community-oriented pollution control agreements with concerned industries may contribute to developing specific and effective programs for detailed environmental regulation and monitoring and compliance methods.

The development of interagency cooperation is the second aspect of Japanese approaches that needs more attention in developing countries. As was the case in industries' adoption of environmental programs, sectoral agencies in Japan resisted early efforts to involve them in environmental management. For example, agencies related to transportation or to industrial investment generally ignored environmental management coordination efforts proposed by the Japan Environment Agency. However, when political consensus was reached on the need for pollution control, both local and national agencies cooperated to support pollution monitoring and abatement programs. Among many other industrial countries and in developing countries especially, administrative and jurisdiction issues remain as constraints to effective interagency environmental programs. The lack of a "culture" of interagency cooperation is a traditional problem, and it will continue to be a major challenge for developing countries in the region to create a working system of consensus-building and coordinated action among government agencies .

Appendix A. Summaries of Reviews of Japanese Case Studies

Case Study on Air Pollution Control in Japan and the Relevance to Developing Countries in East Asia

Indonesia

Reviewer: Rosa Vivien Ratnawati
Head, Division for Environmental Legislation Analysis
Ministry of the Environment, Indonesia

The review highlighted the key similarities and main differences in the experiences of Japan and Indonesia in their efforts to address air pollution.

Similarities in Experiences

The two countries had similar experiences in terms of the link between industrialization and environmental pollution. Japan's rapid industrial development in the 1960s had resulted in serious air pollution problems in several of its major cities. Indonesia experienced major environmental pollution in the 1970s due to the dramatic growth of its industry sector. Total industrial output since 1970 has increased eightfold. Leading industrial nonoil goods manufactured for exports include textiles, garments, plywood and other wood products, electrical goods, footwear, and paper products. Pollution in Indonesia is predicted to increase substantially in the years ahead. By the year 2020, biological oxygen demand (BOD) is estimated to increase tenfold; suspended particulates, fifteenfold; and metal/lead discharges, nineteenfold. In Jakarta the industrial sector presently accounts for about 15 percent of total suspended particulates, 16 percent of nitrogen oxide, and 63 percent of sulfur oxide.

In its efforts to deal with the environmental deterioration of its major cities, Japan changed the focus of national policies from "economic development" through industrial expansion to "pollution control." In a somewhat similar nature, Indonesia set up the "Blue Sky Program" to achieve clean air (particularly in heavily populated urban areas) and to comply with public health standards. The program includes the introduction of unleaded gasoline, gas, and bio-fuels, as well as signed formal agreements between the Ministry of the Environment and industries to reduce emissions. The compliance of industries and state-owned enterprises with environmental standards is sought through enforcement of legislative regulations and the application of nonlegal instruments. For example, industries are rated based on their environmental performance. Clean industries are rated *green*, while those with the worst environmental performance are rated *black*.

The Japanese experience demonstrated that good governance is consequential in achieving a clean, healthy environment. Similarly, Indonesia acknowledges that good governance is important in attaining its environmental goals. The Ministry of the Environment has introduced a "Good Environmental Governance Program." The program's objective is to strengthen local government capacities to enforce regulations with sound environmental considerations and with active participation by the local people.

Japan's overall approach to promoting industries' compliance with environmental standards was based on the concept of "deterrence" or "command and control." The effectiveness of this approach depended not only on the motivation of industries to comply, but also on public environmental awareness and the willingness of people to cooperate and get involved in finding a solution to environmental problems. In Indonesia the Environmental Management Act of 1997 (EMA 1997) is also based on the "deterrence" approach. This act includes provisions for soft loans to assist industries in undertaking pollution abatement investments.

In Indonesia, like in Japan, public pressure has proven to be an effective strategy to settle environmental disputes. A good example is the case of the pulp and paper factory located in Northern Sumatra. Local residents complained that the factory had polluted rivers and caused deforestation. They also complained about the foul odor coming from the factory. Under strong pressure from the local community and nongovernmental organizations, the local government was forced to order the factory to close down.

Differences in Experiences

The above-mentioned similarities between Japan and Indonesia have clear and direct implications for Indonesian efforts to control air pollution. Discussed below are the main differences between these two countries. While differences in situations and experiences are points of deviation and may suggest limits to the applicability of Japan's experience in pollution control to Indonesia, clearly there are important lessons to be learned from these differences.

The Japanese experience showed the importance of political will in addressing pollution concerns. For instance, because of citizens' protests and fear of being voted out of office in favor of leftist politicians, incumbent local government officials had no choice but to enforce stringent emission reduction targets. Indonesia's experience has been quite the opposite. Political will was inadequate at the time when "sustainable development programs" were being implemented, and environmental pollution was never an important political issue. The Ministry of the Environment coordinates various environmental activities in the country. Nonetheless, decisionmaking on environmental issues has not been fully transparent across relevant government agencies, and it often lacks the participation of stakeholders.

According to the case study, once legislative regulations were established in Japan, they were enforced by all relevant government agencies. Such integration of environmental regulations with sectoral department policies would be extremely difficult to implement in Indonesia. Forestry, mining, fisheries, agriculture, and industry are sectors with strong economic interests, and they implement programs without coordination among themselves or with national ministries and local official agencies. Because sectoral policies have not taken into account environmental policies, and vice versa, regulatory enforcement and compliance are weak in Indonesia.

In Japan local government authority to establish and enforce environmental laws, and the capabilities of local officials to do their jobs, were factors that contributed significantly to the control of urban air pollution. In Indonesia major development decisions were made at the central government level; local governments often had little room to make development plans based on local potential and local needs. In recent years Act No. 22/1999 has enabled local governments to formulate their own development plans with input from the local population. In addition, Act No.

25/1999 on Fiscal Balance provides local governments and communities with financial resources and authority to manage their own natural resources for economic development. However, after decades of centralization, there is still an urgent need to strengthen local capacity in order to gain the potential benefits of these laws.

Thailand

Reviewer: Supat Wangwongwatana
Deputy Director-General, Pollution Control Department
Ministry of Science, Technology, and Environment, Bangkok, Thailand

The review evaluated the case study on air pollution control in Japan according to its relevance to Thailand's experience and environmental problems. Considerable similarities were noted between Japan's experience and Thailand's experience in air pollution control management. Certain deviations from the Japanese experience were also mentioned. The salient points raised in the review are as follows:

- The present situation in Thailand with regard to air pollution control is comparable to Japan's experience during the 1950s, when Japan went through the reconstruction of the country after World War II. Thailand today is still recovering from the economic crisis that took place in 1997. Both public and private sector investments in pollution control are less than before the crisis when Thailand was more prosperous. There is concern that imposing pollution control measures on the business community may hinder economic recovery. The demands of daily living are still the major concern for most of the Thai people. Economic development is given a higher priority by the government than pollution control. The latter tends to be accepted only if it complements economic development (for example, eco-tourism).
- Similar to Japan's experience during its early stage of environmental management, the authority for pollution control in Thailand has been contained in numerous laws and dispersed among several governmental ministries for implementation. There are also conflicts of interest between some of the agencies with responsibility for environmental issues. The situation has not improved considerably, even with the enactment in 1992 of the *Enhancement and Conservation of the National Environmental Quality Act*. The act is comparable to Japan's *Basic Law for Pollution Control*. Thailand's law, however, has been weakly enforced, and factories sometimes do not operate their pollution control equipment in order to save operating costs.
- Japan's *Soot and Smoke Control Law* of 1962 and its *Basic Law for Pollution Control* of 1967, which stipulated the need to "undertake living environmental management in harmony with sound industrial development," have similarities with legislation passed in Thailand. Article 32 of the *Enhancement and Conservation of the National Environmental Quality Act* of 1992 gives power to the National Environment Board to prescribe environmental quality standards, including ambient air quality standards. Standards are based not only upon scientific knowledge and principles, but also according to the practicability of such standards from the viewpoint of economic, social, and technological considerations. In Thailand, however, setting stringent standards is not regarded as practicable and realistic.
- Thailand's air pollution problems resemble the air pollution problems in major Japanese cities. Two cases in Thailand are described below.
    The case of the petrochemical complex in the Map Ta Pud District. Thailand's largest petrochemical complex is located in the Map Ta Pud District of Rayong Province. In 1997, when the factories in the complex started full operations, the community situated downwind from

the complex began to complain about an offensive odor caused by various volatile organic compounds (VOCs). Six major factories, including two refineries, were identified to be the sources of VOCs emissions. Children attending the community school located about one kilometer from the petrochemical complex suffered from respiratory illnesses. This problem is similar to the air pollution problem that occurred in Yokkaichi City, Japan, in 1955. The Thai experience is also similar to the case of Kitakyushu City, Japan, in 1970. In Thailand a committee consisting of representatives from national and local government agencies, Thai industries, and the local community was established to implement and monitor air pollution control measures.

The case of a thermal power plant in the Mae Moh District. In 1992 Thailand experienced air pollution caused by sulfur dioxide emissions from the lignite-fired thermal power plant located in the Mae Moh District of Lampang Province. The power plant, with its present installed capacity of 2,625 megawatts, uses lignite with a high sulfur content (3 percent on average), and emissions of sulfur dioxide are not controlled. The average average sulfur dioxide concentration often exceeds 1 part per million (ppm) during the cool months. More than 30 million baths were paid as compensation to the surrounding communities.

The Pollution Control Department in Thailand worked closely with the power plant and the community to conduct a comprehensive study to develop, as an administrative guidance, cost-effective strategies for reducing sulfur dioxide. These actions are similar to the pollution control efforts in Kitakyusha City. The power plant in the Mae Moh District was then required to switch to low-sulfur lignite, to install flue gas desulfurization with 98 percent control efficiency, and to reduce generating load as necessary. The observed sulfur dioxide concentration is now less than 0.15 ppm. A community fund was established by the power plant to improve the quality of life in the community. Nonetheless, three lawsuits have been filed against the power plant, demanding payment of 306 million baths as compensation to pollution victims for accumulated health damages. The outcome of these lawsuits will definitely influence future responses of the business sector to pollution control management.

- In addition to command and control measures, economic incentives similar to those used in Japan are employed in Thailand. Examples are tax reduction to promote investments in pollution control and monitoring equipment, and tax differentiation to promote cleaner technologies. Reduction of personal income tax and corporate tax has never been used. Low-interest loans for pollution control investments are provided to large, medium, and small industries through the Environmental Fund, which is managed by the Industrial Finance Corporation of Thailand. However, low-cost loans are still not very attractive since pollution control enforcement is weak, and the preferential interest rate is not much lower than the commercial rate.
- The involvement of local governments in pollution control is somewhat different in Thailand than in Japan. In Thailand their involvement is quite limited. This is not only because of a lack of authority but also because of a lack of money, expertise, and technical capability. Complaints about air pollution were handled by the national government directly or sometimes indirectly through provincial administration. It was not until the Constitution of 1997 that administrative management and budgetary authority for pollution control started to be delegated from the national government to the local governments. However, lack of expertise and technical capability at the local level is still a major obstacle to decentralized decisionmaking. Environmental engineers in Thailand have not yet been accorded a high status in industrial companies. This is because pollution control measures are usually perceived to affect a company's profitability only indirectly.

- A program to disclose to the public information on industries' pollution control performance is being established in Thailand. The purpose of the program is to raise public awareness of, and public pressure on, polluting industries. As the case of Yokohama City also showed, increased public awareness of environmental problems will induce industries, as well as the government, to improve their performance on pollution control and management.
- In sum, there are a number of similarities between Thailand and Japan with regard to air pollution control management. Thailand has benefited from other countries' experiences, especially Japan's, in dealing with air pollution problems. Thailand has also benefited from international cooperation in improving and speeding up its pollution control program.

Vietnam

Reviewer: Nam Thang Do
Environmental Specialist
Planning and International Relations Division
National Environment Agency

Differences in Experiences

There is a tremendous difference in the time periods when Japan and Vietnam initiated major environmental management activities. Japan paid attention to urban air pollution problems even prior to the 1950s. Citizens' antipollution movements and growing awareness among local residents and the mass media concerning environmental issues had forced governments at the national and local levels to establish pollution control measures and set up ambient environmental quality standards (EQSs). In contrast, environmental pollution was not high on Vietnam's agenda until the early 1990s. Air pollution management in Vietnam came about after the promulgation of the Law on Environmental Protection and the establishment of the Ministry of Science, Technology, and Environment (MOSTE) in 1993.

Dust, predominantly from industrial uses and construction activities, is the most important air pollutant in Vietnam. In the period from 1995 to 2001, monitoring results showed that most urban areas in Vietnam were heavily polluted by dusts. In residential areas close to factories or near major roads, the dust concentration was often two or three times higher than the standards. For instance, the places with the highest levels of dust pollution are residential areas near the Hai Phong cement plant, the VICASA plant in Bien Hoa Province, the Tan Binh industrial zone in Ho Chi Minh City, and the Hon Gai coal plant in Ha Long City.

The industry, transportation, and construction sectors are the major sources of air pollution in Vietnam. Old industries (built before 1975) and especially small and medium-size industries with old production technologies are the worst emitters of air pollutants. Very few of these facilities have scrubber equipment. Most of the old industries ended up within the confines of urban centers during the process of urban expansion. For example, Ho Chi Minh City has about 700 factories; 500 of them are located in urban areas. In Hanoi 200 out of 300 factories in the country's capital are located in urban areas.

With urban and industrial expansion the number of motor vehicles has increased sharply in Vietnam's major cities. Before the 1980s, 80 percent to 90 percent of urban residents used bicycles. Today 80 percent of urban residents use motorcycles. The number of registered motorcycles in Vietnam has increased at an annual rate of 15 percent to 18 percent. Vehicle emissions are particularly troublesome in large cities such as Hanoi, Ho Chi Minh City, Hai Phong, and Da Nang.

Construction activities, which are taking place everywhere and particularly in the urban centers, have generated serious dust pollution. Monitoring results show that 60 percent to 70 percent of dust volume in urban air is from construction.

Vietnam has inadequate enforcement capacity, especially at the local level. Its environmental inspection service was established in 1994, and now sixty out of sixty-one provinces in the country have an environmental inspection division under the Department of Science, Technology, and Environment or DOSTE. (The Ministry of Science, Technology, and Environment is at the national level; DOSTE is a department within each province.) These inspection divisions, however, are understaffed, which makes it difficult for them to undertake the tasks of monitoring and enforcing environmental compliance. Thus many environmental violations have been reported by residents in nearby factories and not by the inspection service.

Similarities in Experiences

Traditional cooperation between the local government, local residents, and the business community played a key role in controlling pollution in Japan's Osaka City. Vietnam also attaches importance to cooperative relationships, and its experience in dealing successfully with pollution problems caused by the Phailai thermal power plant has similarities with Osaka City's experience.

A state-owned enterprise, the Phailai plant was established in 1960 to supply electricity to eight provinces in the Red River Delta in North Vietnam. Its facilities were outdated and inefficient, and although the plant was causing serious air pollution in the area, its continued operation was needed to meet the growing demand for electricity. In the mid-1990s, citizens' complaints about plant emissions became more frequent and vocal. Citizens asked DOSTE and the National Environment Agency (NEA) to take action and close down the plant. In response to these protests, NEA conducted plant inspections, collected data on the environmental and health consequences of plant emissions, and organized negotiations based on a "participatory approach" that involved local residents, power sector personnel, government officials, and the mass media. Through these efforts, power plant officials agreed to (a) comply with the Law on Environmental Protection; (b) invest 12 billion VND in new dust precipitators; and (c) pay 900 million VND to affected people. In Vietnam, as in Japan, three factors working together resulted in effective control of pollution: public pressure and cooperation, the political will to enforce regulations, and the commitment of enterprise to comply with environmental regulations.

Scientific knowledge and monitoring data are crucial aspects of enforcing environmental compliance. Vietnam now has twenty environmental monitoring stations nationwide. Yokohama City successfully resolved its pollution problems largely through pollution control agreements. Vietnam's experience in controlling urban air pollution is largely based on compliance with Environmental Impact Assessment (EIA) requirements. As stipulated in Vietnam's Law of Environmental Protection, both new and old facilities are required to submit EIA reports for review and approval by the Department of Science, Technology, and Environment. EIA reports should include (1) an assessment of the facilities' potential environmental impacts and (2) proposed measures to mitigate adverse effects. All proposed mitigation measures should be undertaken upon approval of the EIA reports.

The "EIA tool," which closely resembles the "command and control" approach to pollution control used in Japan, has been successful in abating pollution in many industrial facilities in Vietnam. A good example is the case of the Ninhbinh thermal power plant, which uses coal. In December 1995, MOSTE chaired a public meeting to discuss means to solve the air pollution problems caused by the plant. It was agreed during the meeting that by the first quarter of 1996, the plant would submit an EIA report. On April 1996 another meeting took place to review the plant's EIA report, and the following agreements were reached:

- Pollution mitigation measures would be implemented within an eighteen-month period.
- During the implementation process, the plant would identify and carry out priority measures as approved by Ninhbinh's Department of Science, Technology, and Environment.

- The plant would be permitted to continue operations, subject to adequate implementation of approved pollution mitigation measures.

The Ministry of Industry approved a budget of 75 billion VND in order to raise the emission stacks in the plant to 140 meters and to install a dust precipitator with an efficiency of 98 to 99 percent. These actions decreased remarkably the level of dust pollution in the town of Ninhbinh from twenty times higher than the standards to permissible levels.

Like Japan, Vietnam has experienced great difficulties in dealing with the worst polluters. In 1999 Vietnam's prime minister directed MOSTE to establish a national program to deal with the worst polluters in a "radical" manner. Two years later MOSTE submitted a proposed program that would reduce pollution considerably by the year 2010, and it identified the top 4,295 polluters in the country. The program would be implemented in two phases. Phase I, covering the 2001-2005 period, would involve regulation of the 465 most serious polluters: 292 production facilities, 87 hospitals, 16 pesticide storage houses, and 3 warfare chemical contaminated sites. Regulation of the production facilities would mostly entail technological improvements and installation of waste treatment systems; other facilities would be required to relocate or close down. Phase II, covering the period from 2006 to 2010, would apply similar regulations to 3,830 facilities nationwide causing pollution to a lesser degree. However, because of the complexity of the matter, the prime minister had still not approved the program by early 2003.

Conclusion

Despite certain differences in how they manage air pollution, Vietnam and Japan have had experiences that share these common features: cooperation among the local governments, businesses, and local citizens on environmental concerns; use of pollution control agreements, and special methods for dealing with serious polluters. Pollution control and environmental management are challenging tasks that require commitments from all sectors of society. Experience should be exchanged between countries to improve pollution control management and thereby contribute to a better environment for all people.

Case Study on Water Pollution Control and Standards in Japan and the Relevance to Developing Countries in East Asia

Indonesia

Reviewer: Indra Mufardi Roesli
Head
City of Bogor Environmental Management Office
Bogor, Indonesia

Industrial pollution control in Japan was assessed in terms of its similarity and relevance to Indonesia. The highlights of the review are as follows:

- Japan has had a long history of industrialization and environmental management. In Indonesia, however, controlling industrial pollution became an important concern only in the 1990s. It was during that decade that several of Indonesia's environmental regulations were enacted. In particular, a comprehensive environmental law was issued in 1997 to deal with industrial pollution at the national level.
- During the late 1990s, the Indonesian political system was transformed from a centralized form of government to a decentralized form of government. Based on the 1997 environmental

law, local governments were granted authority to carry out their own environmental management plans. In addition, the mass media and nongovernmental organizations attained increased freedom to get involved with industrial pollution control issues at the local level. Environmental compliance by industries to control pollution became an important subject of public interest.

- Indonesia's and Japan's experiences with groundwater pollution are vaguely similar. In 1999 the governor of West Java issued an industrial effluent standard that was more stringent than the national standard. Several industries are located in West Java, and the province is one of the most densely populated in the whole country. The concentration of industries and people in West Java resulted in a high degree of pollution of the Citarum River and necessitated stringent measures.
- Pollution control at the provincial level in Indonesia has been conducted by the Provincial Environmental Management Office since 2000. It involves the big Citarum River, which flows from the Bandung region to the Java Sea. This pollution control activity is mainly limited to monitoring the degree of water pollution along the river basin. Monitoring results showed that pollution was significant, and industries were the major polluters. It has been difficult to apprehend and punish polluters because of weak law enforcement.
- West Java had a case of groundwater contamination. Petrol was accidentally spilled when a ground tank in a petrol station in Bogor was being filled. The groundwater contamination lasted for several months. The local community received compensation payments from the petrol industry. This case is similar to the case of RK Excel, a metal-plating industry in Japan that compensated victims. Unlike RK Excel, however, the petrol industry in Bogor was not required by law to undertake clean-up measures. Perhaps this was because the petrol contamination was relatively less significant in scale.
- Japan's experience in industrial pollution control has potentially useful applications to Indonesia. The case study of RK Excel in the Shiga Prefecture underlines the importance of monitoring, quick response, and technology adoption in pollution control.

Philippines

Reviewer: Ruben D. Almendras
Chairman of the Board
Metropolitan Cebu Water District
Cebu City, Philippines

The review evaluated the relevance of Japan's experience in industrial pollution control to developing countries. It reached these two general conclusions:

- Environmental consciousness is directly related to the economic and educational status of the general public. Consequently, in poor countries with low per capita income, government intervention in pollution control and strict enforcement of environmental standards are needed.
- Developing countries generally assign a low priority to environmental management because of limited financial resources. Therefore, it is important that industrial countries require their industries operating in poor countries to comply with environmental standards similar to those implemented in industrial countries.

The main points raised in the review concerning the relevance of industrial pollution control in Japan to the Philippines are as follows:

- Rapid economic and population growth, along with significant changes in land and resource utilization, came to the Province of Cebu in the mid-1980s and put tremendous pressure on the local environment. Population pressures contributed to organic pollution, and industrialization contributed to toxic pollution of water bodies.

- Organic pollution had become irreversible in the downtown area of Cebu. The Metropolitan Cebu Water District (MCWD) wells in the midtown areas that were slightly affected were auto-chlorinated for bacterial contamination. Extremely affected wells were abandoned, and new wells in the upper areas were developed. Cebu's experience, as well as Japan's less than successful efforts to handle organic pollution, indicate the need to address organic pollution of water bodies in terms of population dispersal.

- The Province of Cebu experienced toxic contamination of groundwater involving hexavalent chromium caused by a metal-plating industry. This case resembles the case of RK Excel in the Shiga Prefecture. In the Cebu case, however, the provincial water company (MCWD) discovered the toxic pollution of one of its production wells quite soon, while the degree of pollution was still relatively minor. Thus, the water standard (0.05 milligrams per liter) was restored within a year's time.

- This toxic contamination incident in the Philippines was brought to the attention of government agencies, local governments, local businesses, and the mass media. The polluting company was forced to comply with environmental regulations and treat its chromium discharge because of pressures from the government and community as a whole. The Cebu Metal Treatment Facility that was built in response to the problem was constructed with funding from the government of Germany.

- MCWD has been continuously monitoring all of its productions wells for contamination. The polluting company has been required by law to relocate to a place about 25 kilometers away from its original location.

- Except for water pollution standards, enforcement of environmental standards and regulations in the Philippines is quite irregular. Inspection, monitoring, and enforcement are spotty, and done only when there are complaints from the public.

- Local governments have limited authority to enforce environmental laws. Consequently, the mass media play a key role in exerting pressure on polluting companies to comply with legislative regulations.

Case Study on Japan's Environmental Soft Loan Program and the Relevance to Developing Countries in East Asia

Indonesia

Reviewer: Budi Widianarko
Professor, Head of Graduate Program on Environment and Urban Studies
Soegijaparanata Catholic University (UNIKA)
Semarang, Indonesia

The review identified (a) the important features of Japan's environmental soft loan program that may be relevant to developing countries; (b) the conditions that have influenced the success of Japan's environmental soft loan program; and (c) the potential applicability of soft loan programs to developing countries. The perspective of developing countries was discussed in the context of Indonesia.

The Japanese experience is a special case because of factors inherent within its society. Environmental soft loan programs can clearly help developing countries achieve pollution reductions at reduced costs. However, there are certain preconditions that developing countries need to meet before an environmental soft loan program can be implemented successfully. The review identified the differences between Japan and developing countries and the implications of those differences for achieving a successful soft loan program.

Features of Japan's Program and their Relevance to Developing Countries

In Japan large sums are available for environmental soft loans from domestic sources, such as postal savings and pension funds. In Indonesia, funding for environmental soft loan programs comes from foreign financial institutions like OECF (in Japan) and KfW (in Germany).

Major public financial institutions are engaged in the execution of Japan's environmental soft loan program. The Japan Development Bank (JDB) lends to big businesses; the Japan Financial Corporation for Small Business (JFCSB) and the Japan Environment Corporation (JEC) extend soft loans largely to small and medium-size enterprises. In contrast, Indonesia has a less organized and less focused system for executing its environmental soft loan programs. Indonesia does not have a specific financial institution that is designated to lend soft loan funds. Instead, the Central Bank will ask banks to distribute soft loans when funds become available from abroad, or, in the case of environmental loan funds from KfW, provincial development banks and commercial banks are appointed as executing institutions.

In Japan soft loans are intended to cover only the capital expenditures of pollution abatement investments. In developing countries soft loan programs may cover operation and maintenance expenses. In addition, environmental training of industry personnel will be important to build capacities for dealing with environmental concerns in poor countries.

To the extent that Japan's environmental soft loans are technology based rather than performance based, investments in "standard" technologies are oriented toward "end-of-pipe technologies." At the time when Japan's environmental soft loan program was initially launched, public outcry demanded a quick solution to local pollution problems. End-of-pipe technologies satisfied the immediate needs of the time. Developing clean production technologies would have taken longer to respond to the public's demands for a cleaner environment. From the viewpoint of developing countries today, investments in clean production technologies are more favored than end-of-pipe technologies. This preference reduces the possibility that obsolete pollution control technologies already abandoned in developed countries will find their way to developing countries through technical assistance lending programs financed by foreign capital.

Conditions Contributing to the Success of Japan's Program

Increased public awareness of the quality of the environment forced the Japanese government to take necessary measures to combat industrial pollution. In developing countries, where large numbers of people are preoccupied with their economic survival, environmental quality is less of a priority. The public's awareness of environmental issues is yet to grow in these countries.

Japan introduced its environmental soft loan program after setting up new regulations and tightening standards. The program was designed as a means to reduce companies' financial burden in complying with the new regulations. Indeed, the implementation of the soft loan program was part of an integrated environmental policy.

Effective monitoring is probably the most important condition for ensuring a successful environmental soft loan program. In Japan local governments have been very effective in carrying out monitoring tasks to determine if industries are actually in compliance with the local environmental regulations. Local governments in Japan are also involved in approving soft loan proposals by evaluating if the investment is, in fact, needed. In many developing countries, however, good environmental governance is still at a discussion stage. Accountability is one of the most important components of good environmental governance. Without accountability, monitoring of industries' compliance with regulations is difficult to conduct.

Potential Applicability of Environmental Soft Loan Programs to Developing Countries

Strict enforcement of environmental regulations by the local and national governments, together with strong public support for a clean environment, are the key reasons for Japan's tremendous improvements in environmental quality over time. In many developing countries, however, the opposite actually holds: the public lacks awareness of the need for pollution control, and regulatory enforcement mechanisms are generally weak. It is thus unlikely that the implementation of environmental management measures, such as an environmental soft loan program, can be successful in the absence of strong enforcement. The lack of public environmental awareness is a primary reason for the weak enforcement of environmental regulations.

Successful implementation of an environmental soft loan program requires access to pollution technology; both *engineering know-how* and *trained personnel* are needed. Gaining access to new pollution technology represents a great challenge for developing countries. There is a shortage of locally developed pollution control or clean production technologies. Therefore, developing countries must bear the costs of importing these technologies. This may ultimately lead to a very expensive program.

Environmental monitoring plays a key role in achieving a successful soft loan program. In Japan monitoring is the responsibility of local governments, and it is being carried out with the generous support of local communities. For this to take place elsewhere, monitoring capacities and regulatory enforcement at the local level of government should be established, citizens' participation in environmental management should be promoted, and accountability should be built into the system. Developing countries have much to learn from the Japanese experience.

China

Reviewer: Jianyu Zhang
Program Manager
Environmental Defense China Program
Beijing, China

The review listed similarities and differences between environmental management in Japan (for example, its soft loan program) and China. They are as follows:

- Both the Japanese and Chinese governments realize that a financial mechanism to support environmental improvement projects is important in addition to public awareness of environmental issues, legislative regulation, and enforcement.
- Unlike Japan's soft loan program that is funded through long-term and low-interest loans, China's environmental funds are partly derived from fees collected from polluters. In other words, the Chinese system (PLS) is based on the "Polluter Pays Principle." Japan's soft loan program is not based on this principle and therefore may not achieve an economically efficient solution to environmental concerns.
- Both the Japanese and Chinese systems do not establish a strong linkage between finance and environmental performance.
- Unlike Japan, China does not have designated financial institutions to implement an environmental soft loan program.
- Japan's soft loan program was established as a quick solution to address environmental pollution, and it was socially necessary at the time. Although the program could be stable

over the long run, if the market interest rate dropped, the program could be limited in providing assistance to industries. In China reform of its PLS system, including increased pollution charges, will be implemented soon. There are other new initiatives that are being considered (for example, emissions trading, environmental taxes, discount), and coordination may be a problem.

- There should be a balance between efficiency and a framework to get things done. The key is enforcement and noncompliance penalties. Japan has chosen a results-oriented approach, and it works. But what about the other East Asian countries? Can they follow Japan's path? For China, the answer is probably no.